MASTERING MACHINE LEARNING

Mastering Machine Learning

Dr. Hesham Mohamed Elsherif

ELDON-USA Publishing

Contents

ABOUT THE AUTHOR   1

PREFACE   3

WHO SHOULD READ THIS BOOK?   5

WHY THIS BOOK IS AN ESSENTIAL READING?   7

Chapter 1: Introduction to Machine Learning   9

Chapter 2: Foundations of Programming Languages   70

Chapter 3: Understanding Machine Learning Libraries   132

Chapter 4: Fundamentals of Data Preprocessing   148

Chapter 5: Supervised Learning Algorithms   160

Chapter 6: Unsupervised Learning Algorithms   177

Chapter 7: Deep Learning Basics   192

Chapter 8: Advanced Topics in Machine Learning   207

Chapter 9: Model Evaluation and Hyperparameter Tuning   225

Chapter 10: Real-world Applications and Case Studies   249

Chapter 11: Ethical Considerations in Machine Learning   263

Chapter 12: Future Trends in Machine Learning   275

APPENDICES   288

ABOUT THE AUTHOR

Mastering Machine Learning
A Comprehensive Guide to Language and Practice
BY
Dr. Hesham Mohamed Elsherif

Dr. Hesham Mohamed Elsherif stands at the forefront of library management and research, boasting an impressive 22-year tenure in the field. Holding dual doctoral degrees, one in Management and Organizational Leadership and the other in Information Systems and Technology, Dr. Elsherif brings a unique blend of knowledge to any intellectual endeavor.

An expert in Empirical research methodology, Dr. Elsherif specializes particularly in the Qualitative approach and Action research. This specialization has not only strengthened his research endeavors but has also allowed him to contribute invaluable insights and advancements in these areas.

Over the years, Dr. Elsherif has made significant contributions to the academic world not only as a professional researcher but also as an Adjunct Professor. This multifaceted role in the educational landscape has further solidified his reputation as a thought leader and pioneer.

Furthermore, Dr. Elsherif's expertise isn't confined to one region. He has served as a consultant to numerous educational institutions on an international scale, sharing best practices, innovative strategies, and his deep insights into the ever-evolving realms of management and technology.

Combining a passion for education with an unparalleled depth of knowledge, Dr. Elsherif continues to inspire, educate, and lead in both the library and academic communities.

PREFACE

Welcome to "Mastering Machine Learning: A Comprehensive Guide to Language and Practice." In today's rapidly evolving technological landscape, the ability to harness the power of machine learning has become paramount. Whether you're a seasoned programmer looking to delve into the intricacies of artificial intelligence or a newcomer eager to explore the realm of data-driven decision-making, this book is your gateway to mastering the language of machine learning.

Machine learning, with its ability to extract insights from vast amounts of data and make predictions with remarkable accuracy, has revolutionized countless industries, from healthcare to finance, from retail to transportation. However, mastering machine learning entails more than just understanding algorithms and writing code. It requires a solid foundation in programming languages, a deep understanding of mathematical concepts, and a keen intuition for problem-solving.

This book is designed to be your comprehensive companion on this journey of discovery. From the fundamentals of programming languages to the intricacies of deep learning, each chapter is crafted to provide you with the knowledge and skills necessary to navigate the complex landscape of machine learning. Whether you're interested in supervised learning algorithms, unsupervised learning techniques, or the latest advancements in deep learning, you'll find a wealth of information to guide you along the way.

But this book is more than just a collection of theories and algorithms. It's a hands-on guide that empowers you to apply what you've learned to real-world problems. With practical examples, code snippets, and case studies, you'll learn not only how to build machine learning models but also how to evaluate their performance, fine-tune their parameters, and deploy them in production environments.

Moreover, as we explore the fascinating world of machine learning, we cannot ignore the ethical implications of our work. From concerns about bias and fairness to questions of privacy and security, this book encourages you to consider the ethical dimensions of machine learning and to approach your work with integrity and responsibility.

Whether you're a student, a researcher, a data scientist, or simply a curious mind eager to explore the frontiers of artificial intelligence, "Mastering Machine Learning" is your guidebook to unlocking the full potential of machine learning. So, dive in, embrace the challenges, and embark on this exhilarating journey into the heart of machine intelligence.

Happy learning!

Dr. Hesham Mohamed Elsherif

WHO SHOULD READ THIS BOOK?

"Mastering Machine Learning: A Comprehensive Guide to Language and Practice" is intended for a diverse audience of individuals interested in exploring the fascinating field of machine learning. Whether you are a novice programmer, a seasoned data scientist, or an industry professional seeking to expand your skill set, this book offers valuable insights and practical knowledge to suit your needs.

1. **Students:** Whether you're pursuing a degree in computer science, engineering, mathematics, or any other related field, this book serves as an invaluable resource for understanding the principles and techniques of machine learning. With its clear explanations and hands-on examples, students at all levels will find this book to be an indispensable companion in their academic journey.

2. **Professionals Transitioning into Data Science:** Are you looking to transition into a career in data science or artificial intelligence? This book provides a solid foundation in programming languages, statistical concepts, and machine learning algorithms, making it the perfect starting point for professionals seeking to enter the world of data-driven decision-making.

3. **Data Scientists and Analysts:** For experienced data scientists and analysts, this book offers a comprehensive overview of advanced machine learning techniques, including deep

learning, reinforcement learning, and natural language processing. Whether you're looking to enhance your existing skills or explore new avenues of research, you'll find valuable insights and practical guidance to help you stay ahead in this rapidly evolving field.

4. **Software Engineers and Developers:** Machine learning is increasingly becoming an integral part of software development, enabling developers to build intelligent applications and systems. This book equips software engineers and developers with the knowledge and tools they need to integrate machine learning into their projects, from basic algorithms to sophisticated models.

5. **Researchers and Academics:** If you're involved in research or academia, this book provides a solid foundation for understanding the theoretical underpinnings of machine learning, as well as practical techniques for applying machine learning to real-world problems. With its in-depth coverage of both fundamental concepts and cutting-edge advancements, this book serves as a valuable reference for researchers and academics in the field of artificial intelligence.

In summary, "Mastering Machine Learning" is a versatile resource that caters to the diverse needs and interests of students, professionals, researchers, and enthusiasts alike. Whether you're looking to build your foundational knowledge, expand your skill set, or stay abreast of the latest developments in machine learning, this book is essential reading for anyone interested in unlocking the potential of artificial intelligence.

WHY THIS BOOK IS AN ESSENTIAL READING?

In the age of data-driven decision-making and artificial intelligence, proficiency in machine learning is no longer just an asset—it's a necessity. "Mastering Machine Learning: A Comprehensive Guide to Language and Practice" is essential reading for anyone looking to thrive in this rapidly evolving landscape. Here's why:

1. **Foundation Building:** This book lays a solid foundation in the fundamental concepts and techniques of machine learning, making it accessible to beginners while also providing valuable insights for advanced practitioners. From programming languages to mathematical principles, readers will gain a comprehensive understanding of the building blocks of machine learning.

2. **Practical Application:** Unlike theoretical textbooks that focus solely on concepts, this book emphasizes practical application. Through hands-on examples, code snippets, and real-world case studies, readers learn how to apply machine learning algorithms to solve practical problems, from image recognition to natural language processing.

3. **Comprehensive Coverage:** "Mastering Machine Learning" covers a wide range of topics, including supervised and unsupervised learning algorithms, deep learning, model evaluation, and ethical considerations. Whether you're interested in

classification, regression, clustering, or reinforcement learning, you'll find everything you need to know within these pages.

4. **Up-to-Date Information:** Machine learning is a rapidly evolving field, with new algorithms, techniques, and tools emerging constantly. This book incorporates the latest advancements in machine learning, ensuring that readers stay abreast of the cutting-edge developments in the field.

5. **Versatility:** Whether you're a student, a professional, a researcher, or an enthusiast, this book caters to a diverse audience with varying levels of expertise. Beginners will find clear explanations and step-by-step guidance, while experienced practitioners will appreciate the depth of coverage and practical insights.

6. **Ethical Considerations:** In addition to technical knowledge, this book also addresses the ethical implications of machine learning, including issues of bias, fairness, privacy, and accountability. By fostering a deeper understanding of the ethical dimensions of AI, readers are equipped to approach their work with integrity and responsibility.

In conclusion, "Mastering Machine Learning" is not just a book—it's a roadmap to success in the field of artificial intelligence. Whether you're looking to launch a career in data science, enhance your existing skills, or simply satisfy your curiosity about the inner workings of intelligent systems, this book is essential reading for anyone interested in unlocking the full potential of machine learning.

Enjoy Learning!!

Dr. Hesham Mohamed Elsherif

Chapter 1: Introduction to Machine Learning

Machine learning represents a pivotal paradigm shift in how computers can learn from data to improve performance on tasks without being explicitly programmed. In this introductory section, we delve into the essence of machine learning, its importance, and the various types that underpin its vast applications.

What is Machine Learning?

Machine learning is a subset of artificial intelligence (AI) that focuses on the development of algorithms and statistical models that enable computers to perform tasks without explicit instructions, relying on patterns and inference instead. It encompasses a diverse set of techniques and approaches, ranging from simple linear regression to complex deep neural networks.

At its core, machine learning revolves around the concept of learning from data. By analyzing and processing large datasets, machines can identify patterns, extract meaningful insights, and make predictions or decisions based on this acquired knowledge. This ability to learn from data is what distinguishes machine learning from traditional rule-based programming approaches.

Machine learning is a subset of artificial intelligence (AI) that enables computers to learn from data and improve their performance on tasks without being explicitly programmed. It involves the development of algorithms and models that can recognize patterns, make predictions, and derive insights from data, thereby enabling intelligent decision-making and automation across various domains. Let's delve into the essence of machine learning with in-depth explanations and live examples:

1.Understanding the Concept:

Machine learning revolves around the concept of learning from data. Instead of following predefined rules or instructions, machines are trained to identify patterns and relationships within datasets, allowing them to generalize and make predictions on new, unseen data.

2.Core Components of Machine Learning:

Data:

At the heart of machine learning is data. Datasets consist of input features (attributes) and corresponding output labels (target variables). The quality, quantity, and relevance of data profoundly impact the performance and accuracy of machine learning models.

Data serves as the lifeblood of machine learning, providing the raw material from which algorithms learn and derive insights.

1. **Importance of Data:**

   Data is the foundation upon which machine learning algorithms operate. It encompasses a wide range of information, including observations, measurements, images, text, and more. The quality, quantity, and relevance of data profoundly influence the performance and effectiveness of machine learning models. Without sufficient and high-quality data, machine learning algorithms may struggle to generalize well to new, unseen instances.

2. **Types of Data:**

   Data in machine learning can be classified into various types, each with its own characteristics and properties:

   Structured Data: Structured data is organized into a tabular format with well-defined rows and columns. Examples include databases, spreadsheets, and CSV files. Structured data is commonly used in supervised learning tasks such as classification and regression.

Unstructured Data: Unstructured data lacks a predefined data model or organization. Examples include text documents, images, audio recordings, and video streams. Unstructured data presents unique challenges for machine learning algorithms but also offers rich opportunities for extracting valuable insights through techniques such as natural language processing (NLP) and computer vision.

Semi-Structured Data: Semi-structured data falls somewhere between structured and unstructured data. It may have some organizational properties, such as tags or labels, but lacks the strict schema of structured data. Examples include JSON, XML, and HTML files. Semi-structured data is common in web scraping, data mining, and data integration tasks.

3. **Data Preprocessing:**

Data preprocessing is a critical step in the machine learning pipeline, where raw data is cleaned, transformed, and prepared for analysis. This process helps to address common challenges such as missing values, outliers, noise, and inconsistencies in the data. Key techniques in data preprocessing include:

Data Cleaning: Removing or correcting errors, inconsistencies, and irrelevant information from the dataset.

Feature Scaling: Scaling numerical features to a standard range (e.g., normalization or standardization) to ensure that they contribute equally to the learning process.

Feature Encoding: Converting categorical features into numerical representations (e.g., one-hot encoding) suitable for machine learning algorithms.

Dimensionality Reduction: Reducing the number of features in the dataset while preserving relevant information (e.g., principal component analysis or feature selection).

4. **Data Splitting:**

To evaluate the performance of machine learning models effectively, the dataset is typically divided into training, validation, and test sets:

Training Set: The training set is used to train the machine learning model, allowing it to learn patterns and relationships in the data.

Validation Set: The validation set is used to fine-tune model hyperparameters and assess performance during training, helping to prevent overfitting.

Test Set: The test set is used to evaluate the final performance of the trained model on unseen data, providing an unbiased estimate of its generalization ability.

Data is the cornerstone of machine learning, providing the raw material from which algorithms learn and make predictions. By understanding the types of data, the importance of data preprocessing, and the role of data splitting, practitioners can effectively leverage data to build accurate and robust machine learning models. In the next sections, we will explore the other core components of machine learning, including models, algorithms, and evaluation techniques.

Model:

A model is a mathematical representation or algorithm that learns patterns from data. It encapsulates the relationship between input features and output labels, enabling the machine to make predictions or decisions.

In the realm of machine learning, models serve as the mathematical representations or algorithms that learn from data to make predictions or decisions. Understanding the core components of models is essential for grasping the intricacies of machine learning.

1. **Model Representation:**

   A machine learning model is a mathematical function that maps input features to output predictions or labels. The choice of model representation depends on the nature of the problem and the characteristics of the data. Common model representations include:

Linear Models: Linear models assume a linear relationship between input features and output predictions. Examples include linear regression for regression tasks and logistic regression for binary classification tasks.

Non-linear Models: Non-linear models capture more complex relationships between input features and output predictions. Examples include decision trees, support vector machines (SVMs), and neural networks.

Ensemble Models: Ensemble models combine multiple base models to improve predictive performance. Examples include random forests, gradient boosting machines (GBMs), and ensemble neural networks.

2. **Model Training:**

Model training is the process of adjusting the parameters or structure of the model to minimize errors and improve performance on the training data. This process involves optimization techniques such as gradient descent, which iteratively updates the model parameters to minimize a loss function that quantifies the difference between predicted and actual values.

During training, the model learns from the training data by adjusting its parameters to minimize the discrepancy between predicted and actual values. The goal is to find the optimal set of parameters that best represent the underlying patterns and relationships in the data.

3. **Model Evaluation:**

Model evaluation is the process of assessing the performance of the trained model on unseen data to determine its effectiveness and generalization ability. Common evaluation metrics vary depending on the type of machine learning task:

For regression tasks, metrics such as mean squared error (MSE) or root mean squared error (RMSE) quantify the difference between predicted and actual values.

For classification tasks, metrics such as accuracy, precision, recall,

F1 score, and area under the receiver operating characteristic (ROC) curve measure the model's performance in predicting class labels.

Cross-validation techniques, such as k-fold cross-validation, are often used to assess the robustness and reliability of the model across different subsets of the data.

4. **Model Deployment:**

Once trained and evaluated, the final step is deploying the model into production to make predictions or decisions on new, unseen data. Model deployment involves integrating the trained model into existing systems or applications, ensuring scalability, reliability, and real-time performance.

Machine learning models serve as the backbone of predictive analytics, enabling computers to learn from data and make intelligent decisions. By understanding the core components of models, including their representation, training, evaluation, and deployment, practitioners can develop accurate, robust, and scalable machine learning solutions for a wide range of applications. In the next sections, we will explore the algorithms and techniques used to train and optimize machine learning models, further expanding our understanding of the field.

Learning Algorithm:

Learning algorithms are techniques or methods used to train machine learning models. They adjust the model's parameters or structure based on the available data to minimize errors and improve performance.

Learning algorithms are the backbone of machine learning, serving as the engines that drive the process of extracting patterns and insights from data. Understanding the core components of learning algorithms is essential for comprehending how machine learning models are trained and optimized.

1. **Learning Paradigms:**

   Machine learning algorithms can be broadly categorized into three main paradigms based on the type of learning they employ:

   Supervised Learning: In supervised learning, algorithms learn from labeled data, where each example is paired with a corresponding target label or output. The algorithm's objective is to learn a mapping from inputs to outputs, enabling it to make predictions on new, unseen instances. Examples include linear regression for regression tasks and support vector machines (SVMs) for classification tasks.

   Unsupervised Learning: In unsupervised learning, algorithms learn patterns and structures from unlabeled data, without explicit guidance or supervision. The goal is to uncover hidden relationships or groupings within the data. Clustering algorithms, such as k-means clustering and hierarchical clustering, are common examples of unsupervised learning techniques.

   Reinforcement Learning: Reinforcement learning involves learning to make sequential decisions through interaction with an environment. The agent receives feedback in the form of rewards or penalties based on its actions, guiding it towards learning optimal behavior. Reinforcement learning has applications in areas such as robotics, game playing, and autonomous systems.

2. **Optimization Techniques:**

   Learning algorithms often rely on optimization techniques to adjust the parameters or structure of the model and minimize a loss function that quantifies the difference between predicted and actual values. Common optimization techniques include:

   Gradient Descent: Gradient descent is an iterative optimization algorithm that updates the model parameters in the direction of the steepest descent of the loss function. By following the gradient of the loss function, the algorithm converges towards the optimal set of parameters that minimize the loss.

Stochastic Gradient Descent (SGD): SGD is a variant of gradient descent that updates the model parameters using a random subset of training examples (mini-batch) at each iteration. SGD is computationally efficient and well-suited for large-scale datasets. **Adam, RMSprop, and Other Variants:** These are adaptive optimization algorithms that adjust the learning rate dynamically based on the gradient magnitudes. They offer improved convergence speed and stability compared to traditional gradient descent methods.

3. **Regularization Techniques:**

To prevent overfitting and improve the generalization ability of machine learning models, regularization techniques are often employed. Common regularization techniques include:

L1 and L2 Regularization: L1 and L2 regularization penalize large parameter values by adding a regularization term to the loss function. L1 regularization (lasso) encourages sparsity in the model parameters, while L2 regularization (ridge) prevents parameter magnitudes from becoming too large.

Dropout: Dropout is a regularization technique commonly used in neural networks. It randomly drops a fraction of units (neurons) from the network during training, preventing units from relying too heavily on specific features or patterns.

Learning algorithms form the core components of machine learning, enabling computers to learn from data and make intelligent decisions. By understanding the fundamental paradigms, optimization techniques, and regularization methods employed by learning algorithms, practitioners can effectively train, optimize, and deploy machine learning models for a wide range of applications. In the next sections, we will explore specific algorithms and techniques used in supervised learning, unsupervised learning, and reinforcement learning, further expanding our understanding of the field.

Types of Machine Learning:

Supervised Learning:

In supervised learning, the algorithm learns from labeled data, where each input example is associated with a corresponding output label. For example, in a spam email classification task, the algorithm is trained on a dataset containing emails labeled as "spam" or "not spam."

Supervised learning is a fundamental paradigm in machine learning where algorithms learn from labeled data, making it one of the most widely used and studied approaches

1. **Understanding Supervised Learning:**

   In supervised learning, algorithms learn from a labeled dataset, where each example consists of input features and corresponding output labels. The goal is to learn a mapping from inputs to outputs, enabling the algorithm to predict the correct label for new, unseen instances. Supervised learning tasks can be broadly categorized into two main types:

   Classification: Classification tasks involve predicting discrete class labels or categories for input instances. Examples include spam email detection, sentiment analysis, and image classification.

   Regression: Regression tasks involve predicting continuous numerical values for input instances. Examples include predicting house prices based on features such as size, location, and number of bedrooms, and predicting sales revenue based on advertising expenditure.

2. **Supervised Learning Algorithms:**

   Supervised learning encompasses a diverse range of algorithms, each suited to different types of problems and data. Some common supervised learning algorithms include:

   Linear Regression: Linear regression is a simple yet powerful algorithm for regression tasks. It models the relationship between input features and output labels using a linear equation, minimizing the sum of squared errors between predicted and actual values.

Logistic Regression: Logistic regression is a binary classification algorithm that models the probability of an instance belonging to a particular class. It uses the logistic (sigmoid) function to map input features to class probabilities and makes predictions based on a predefined threshold.

Decision Trees: Decision trees are versatile algorithms that can be used for both classification and regression tasks. They partition the feature space into regions based on feature values and make predictions by traversing the tree from the root to the leaf nodes.

Support Vector Machines (SVMs): SVMs are powerful classifiers that aim to find the optimal hyperplane that separates different classes in the feature space. They work by maximizing the margin between classes while minimizing classification errors.

Neural Networks: Neural networks are a class of deep learning algorithms inspired by the structure and function of the human brain. They consist of interconnected layers of neurons (nodes) and are capable of learning complex patterns and relationships from data.

3. **Evaluation Metrics:**

To assess the performance of supervised learning models, various evaluation metrics are used depending on the task at hand. Common evaluation metrics for classification tasks include:

Accuracy: The proportion of correctly classified instances out of the total number of instances.

Precision: The ratio of true positive predictions to the total number of positive predictions, measuring the model's ability to avoid false positives.

Recall: The ratio of true positive predictions to the total number of actual positive instances, measuring the model's ability to capture all positive instances.

F1 Score: The harmonic mean of precision and recall, providing a balanced measure of a model's performance.

For regression tasks, evaluation metrics such as mean squared error (MSE), root mean squared error (RMSE), and mean absolute error (MAE) are commonly used to quantify the difference between predicted and actual values.

Supervised learning is a powerful paradigm in machine learning, enabling algorithms to learn from labeled data and make predictions or decisions on new, unseen instances. By understanding the concepts, algorithms, and evaluation methods of supervised learning, practitioners can build accurate and robust models for a wide range of classification and regression tasks. In the next sections, we will explore other types of machine learning, including unsupervised learning and reinforcement learning, further expanding our understanding of the field.

Unsupervised Learning:

Unsupervised learning involves learning patterns and structures from unlabeled data. The algorithm seeks to identify inherent relationships or groupings within the data without explicit guidance. An example is clustering similar documents based on their content.

Unsupervised learning represents a powerful paradigm in machine learning where algorithms learn patterns and structures from unlabeled data, without explicit guidance or supervision.

1. **Understanding Unsupervised Learning:**

   Unsupervised learning involves learning patterns and structures from data without the presence of explicit labels or target outputs. Unlike supervised learning, where the algorithm is provided with labeled examples, unsupervised learning algorithms must infer the underlying structure of the data on their own. Unsupervised learning tasks can be broadly categorized into two main types:

Clustering: Clustering tasks involve grouping similar instances or data points together based on their inherent similarities or proximity in the feature space. The goal is to partition the data into clusters such that instances within the same cluster are more similar to each other than to instances in other clusters.

Dimensionality Reduction: Dimensionality reduction tasks involve reducing the number of features or dimensions in the data while preserving its essential characteristics and structure. This can help alleviate the curse of dimensionality, improve computational efficiency, and facilitate visualization and interpretation of high-dimensional data.

2. **Unsupervised Learning Algorithms:**

Unsupervised learning encompasses a diverse range of algorithms, each tailored to different types of unsupervised learning tasks. Some common unsupervised learning algorithms include:

K-Means Clustering: K-means clustering is a popular algorithm for partitioning data into k clusters based on their feature similarity. It iteratively assigns data points to the nearest cluster centroid and updates the centroids until convergence.

Hierarchical Clustering: Hierarchical clustering builds a hierarchy of clusters by recursively merging or splitting clusters based on their pairwise distances or similarities. It can produce dendrograms that visualize the hierarchical structure of the data.

Principal Component Analysis (PCA): PCA is a dimensionality reduction technique that transforms high-dimensional data into a lower-dimensional space while preserving as much variance as possible. It identifies the principal components (linear combinations of the original features) that capture the most significant variation in the data.

t-Distributed Stochastic Neighbor Embedding (t-SNE): t-SNE is a nonlinear dimensionality reduction technique that emphasizes local relationships between data points in high-dimensional space. It is particularly useful for visualizing high-dimensional data in two or three dimensions.

3. **Evaluation Metrics:**

Evaluating the performance of unsupervised learning algorithms can be challenging due to the absence of ground truth labels. However, various evaluation metrics and techniques can be used to assess the quality of clustering or dimensionality reduction results, including:

Silhouette Score: The silhouette score measures the cohesion and separation of clusters, providing a quantitative measure of cluster quality. It ranges from -1 to 1, with higher values indicating better clustering.

Inertia: Inertia measures the sum of squared distances of data points to their nearest cluster centroids in k-means clustering. Lower inertia values indicate tighter and more compact clusters.

Explained Variance Ratio (PCA): In PCA, the explained variance ratio quantifies the proportion of variance explained by each principal component. It helps assess the amount of information retained after dimensionality reduction.

Unsupervised learning is a powerful paradigm in machine learning, enabling algorithms to uncover hidden patterns and structures in un-labeled data. By understanding the concepts, algorithms, and evaluation methods of unsupervised learning, practitioners can gain insights into the underlying structure of their data and extract valuable knowledge without the need for explicit supervision. In the next sections, we will explore other types of machine learning, including reinforcement learning, further expanding our understanding of the field.

Reinforcement Learning:

Reinforcement learning is a paradigm where an agent learns to make sequential decisions through interaction with an environment. The agent receives feedback in the form of rewards or penalties based on its actions, guiding it towards learning optimal behavior. An example is training an AI agent to play chess or navigate a maze.

Reinforcement learning represents a dynamic paradigm in machine learning where algorithms learn to make sequential decisions through interaction with an environment.

1. **Understanding Reinforcement Learning:**

   Reinforcement learning (RL) is a type of machine learning where an agent learns to achieve a goal or maximize a cumulative reward by taking actions in an environment. Unlike supervised and unsupervised learning, where the algorithm learns from labeled or unlabeled data, reinforcement learning relies on trial and error exploration to discover optimal strategies through interactions with the environment.

2. **Key Components of Reinforcement Learning:**

   Reinforcement learning involves several key components:

   Agent: The agent is the learner or decision-maker that interacts with the environment. It observes the current state of the environment, selects actions based on a policy, and receives feedback or rewards from the environment.

   Environment: The environment is the external system with which the agent interacts. It is defined by a set of states, actions, transition dynamics, and rewards. The environment changes in response to the agent's actions, influencing future states and rewards.

   State: A state represents the current configuration or condition of the environment. It encapsulates all relevant information necessary for decision-making, including the agent's observations, past actions, and environmental dynamics.

   Action: An action represents the decision made by the agent to transition from one state to another. Actions can be discrete or continuous, depending on the nature of the environment and the task.

   Reward: A reward is a scalar feedback signal provided by the environment to the agent after each action. It indicates the immediate benefit or cost associated with the agent's action and serves as a measure of success or failure.

Policy: A policy is a strategy or mapping from states to actions that governs the agent's decision-making process. It defines how the agent selects actions in different states to maximize expected rewards over time.

3. **Reinforcement Learning Algorithms:**

Reinforcement learning encompasses a variety of algorithms for learning optimal policies and value functions. Some common reinforcement learning algorithms include:

Q-Learning: Q-learning is a model-free reinforcement learning algorithm that learns the optimal action-value function (Q-function) through iterative updates based on the Bellman equation. It is well-suited for discrete action spaces and tabular representations.

Deep Q-Networks (DQN): DQN is an extension of Q-learning that uses deep neural networks to approximate the Q-function. It can handle high-dimensional state spaces and has been successfully applied to a wide range of tasks, including playing Atari games and robotic control.

Policy Gradient Methods: Policy gradient methods directly optimize the policy parameterization to maximize expected rewards. Examples include the REINFORCE algorithm and its variants, which use stochastic gradient ascent to update policy parameters based on sampled trajectories.

Actor-Critic Methods: Actor-critic methods combine elements of both value-based and policy-based approaches. They maintain both a policy (actor) and a value function (critic) and use them to guide decision-making and value estimation.

4. **Evaluation and Training:**

Evaluating reinforcement learning algorithms can be challenging due to the dynamic nature of the environment and the long-term nature of rewards. Common evaluation methods include:

Cumulative Reward: Cumulative reward measures the total reward accumulated by the agent over a trajectory or episode. It provides a measure of the agent's performance in achieving its goals.

Exploration vs. Exploitation: Balancing exploration (trying new actions to discover optimal strategies) and exploitation (leveraging known strategies to maximize immediate rewards) is crucial in reinforcement learning. Evaluation metrics such as epsilon-greedy policy exploration rates can assess the agent's ability to balance exploration and exploitation.

Training Stability: Reinforcement learning algorithms often require careful tuning of hyperparameters and exploration strategies to ensure stable and effective learning. Monitoring training curves, convergence behavior, and performance metrics can help assess the stability and effectiveness of training.

5. **Applications of Reinforcement Learning:**

Reinforcement learning has found applications in a wide range of domains, including:

Game Playing: Reinforcement learning algorithms have achieved remarkable success in playing complex games such as chess, Go, and video games. Deep reinforcement learning approaches have surpassed human-level performance in many games.

Robotics: Reinforcement learning is used to train autonomous agents and robots to perform tasks such as manipulation, locomotion, and navigation in real-world environments.

Recommendation Systems: Reinforcement learning algorithms can be used to personalize recommendations and optimize user engagement in online platforms and e-commerce websites.

Finance: Reinforcement learning is applied in algorithmic trading, portfolio management, and risk assessment in financial markets.

Reinforcement learning represents a dynamic and exciting paradigm in machine learning, enabling agents to learn to make sequential decisions through interaction with an environment. By understanding the key components, algorithms, applications, and evaluation methods of reinforcement learning, practitioners can develop intelligent agents capable of learning and adapting to complex environments and tasks. In the next sections, we will explore other types of machine learning, including semi-supervised learning, further expanding our understanding of the field.

4. Real-world Examples:

Image Classification:

A classic example of supervised learning is image classification, where algorithms are trained to recognize objects or patterns within images. For instance, a convolutional neural network (CNN) can be trained on a dataset of labeled images to distinguish between different types of animals, vehicles, or objects.

Image classification is a prominent application of machine learning, where algorithms are trained to analyze and categorize images into predefined classes or categories.

1. **Understanding Image Classification:**

   Image classification involves the process of assigning a label or category to an input image based on its visual content. It is a fundamental computer vision task with applications ranging from medical diagnosis and autonomous driving to content moderation and object recognition.

2. **Techniques and Algorithms:**

   Image classification algorithms leverage various techniques and architectures to learn patterns and features from images. Some common techniques and algorithms include:

   Convolutional Neural Networks (CNNs): CNNs are a class of deep learning architectures specifically designed for processing and analyzing visual data. They consist of multiple layers of convolutional and pooling operations, followed by fully connected layers for classification. CNNs have achieved state-of-the-art performance in image classification tasks due to their ability to capture spatial hierarchies of features.

Transfer Learning: Transfer learning is a technique where pre-trained CNN models are fine-tuned on new datasets or tasks. By leveraging features learned from large-scale datasets such as ImageNet, transfer learning allows practitioners to achieve good performance on image classification tasks with limited labeled data.

Data Augmentation: Data augmentation techniques such as rotation, scaling, cropping, and flipping are used to increase the diversity of training data and improve the generalization ability of image classification models. By generating synthetic variations of input images, data augmentation helps prevent overfitting and improves model robustness.

3. **Real-world Examples:**

Image classification finds applications across a wide range of domains and industries. Some notable real-world examples include:

Medical Imaging: In medical imaging, image classification algorithms are used for diagnosing diseases and abnormalities from medical images such as X-rays, MRI scans, and histopathology slides. For example, CNNs have been employed to detect and classify various types of cancers, including breast cancer, lung cancer, and skin cancer, with high accuracy.

Autonomous Vehicles: Image classification plays a crucial role in autonomous vehicles for detecting and recognizing objects in the vehicle's surroundings. CNN-based models are used to classify objects such as pedestrians, vehicles, traffic signs, and obstacles, enabling safe navigation and decision-making in real-time.

Content Moderation: Social media platforms and online communities use image classification algorithms for content moderation and filtering. These algorithms automatically detect and classify inappropriate or harmful content such as violence, nudity, hate speech, and graphic images, helping maintain a safe and respectful online environment.

Retail and E-commerce: Image classification is used in retail and e-commerce for product categorization, recommendation, and visual search. By analyzing product images, algorithms can automatically categorize products into relevant categories, recommend visually similar items to users, and enable visual search functionality, enhancing the shopping experience.

4. **Challenges and Considerations:**

While image classification has made significant advancements, it still faces several challenges and considerations, including:

Data Quality and Quantity: Image classification models require large amounts of labeled data for training, which can be expensive and time-consuming to collect and annotate. Ensuring the quality and diversity of training data is crucial for building robust and reliable models.

Robustness to Variability: Image classification models must be robust to variations in lighting conditions, camera angles, backgrounds, and object orientations. Robustness to such variability requires careful data preprocessing, augmentation, and model architecture design.

Interpretability and Bias: Deep learning models, particularly CNNs, are often criticized for their lack of interpretability and potential bias. Understanding how models make predictions and addressing biases in training data are essential for building fair and trustworthy image classification systems.

Image classification is a pervasive application of machine learning with diverse real-world applications across industries such as healthcare, autonomous vehicles, content moderation, and retail. By leveraging techniques such as convolutional neural networks, transfer learning, and data augmentation, image classification algorithms can analyze visual data with high accuracy and efficiency, enabling automated decision-making and intelligent systems. In the next sections, we will explore other real-world examples of machine learning applications, further highlighting the breadth and impact of the field.

Predictive Maintenance:

In industrial settings, machine learning is used for predictive maintenance, where algorithms analyze sensor data from machinery to predict equipment failures before they occur. By detecting anomalies or patterns indicative of potential faults, maintenance can be scheduled proactively, minimizing downtime and optimizing productivity.

Predictive maintenance is a proactive approach to maintenance that uses machine learning algorithms to predict when equipment or machinery is likely to fail, enabling timely maintenance and preventing costly downtime.

1. **Understanding Predictive Maintenance:**

   Predictive maintenance aims to predict equipment failures before they occur by analyzing historical data, sensor readings, and other relevant parameters. By identifying early warning signs of equipment degradation or failure, predictive maintenance helps organizations optimize maintenance schedules, minimize downtime, and reduce maintenance costs.

2. **Techniques and Algorithms:**

   Predictive maintenance relies on various machine learning techniques and algorithms to analyze data and make accurate predictions. Some common techniques and algorithms include:

   Machine Learning Models: Supervised learning algorithms such as decision trees, random forests, support vector machines (SVMs), and neural networks are commonly used for predictive maintenance tasks. These models learn patterns and relationships from historical data to predict future failures or maintenance events.

   Time-series Analysis: Time-series analysis techniques such as autoregressive integrated moving average (ARIMA), exponential smoothing, and recurrent neural networks (RNNs) are used to model and forecast time-varying data, such as sensor readings and equipment performance metrics.

Anomaly Detection: Anomaly detection algorithms identify abnormal or anomalous patterns in data that may indicate equipment failures or malfunctions. Techniques such as statistical methods, clustering, and autoencoders are used to detect deviations from normal operating conditions.

Survival Analysis: Survival analysis techniques such as Kaplan-Meier estimation, Cox proportional hazards model, and accelerated failure time (AFT) model are used to analyze time-to-event data and predict the probability of failure at a given point in time.

3. **Real-world Examples:**

Predictive maintenance is widely adopted across industries to optimize asset management and reduce downtime. Some notable real-world examples include:

Manufacturing: In manufacturing plants, predictive maintenance is used to monitor and maintain critical equipment such as motors, pumps, and conveyor belts. By analyzing sensor data and equipment performance metrics, manufacturers can predict equipment failures, schedule maintenance proactively, and avoid costly production disruptions.

Energy: In the energy sector, predictive maintenance is employed to monitor and optimize the performance of power generation and distribution systems. By analyzing data from sensors, meters, and smart grids, energy companies can predict equipment failures, identify energy losses, and improve system reliability and efficiency.

Transportation: In transportation systems such as railways, airlines, and fleets, predictive maintenance is used to monitor and maintain vehicles and infrastructure. By analyzing data from onboard sensors, GPS trackers, and maintenance logs, transportation companies can predict component failures, optimize maintenance schedules, and ensure passenger safety and comfort.

Healthcare: In healthcare facilities, predictive maintenance is used to monitor and maintain medical equipment such as MRI machines, X-ray machines, and ventilators. By analyzing equipment usage patterns, sensor data, and maintenance records, healthcare providers can predict equipment failures, schedule preventive maintenance, and ensure uninterrupted patient care.

4. **Challenges and Considerations:**

Despite its benefits, predictive maintenance faces several challenges and considerations, including:

Data Quality and Availability: Predictive maintenance relies on high-quality, reliable data for accurate predictions. Ensuring data quality, completeness, and availability can be challenging, especially in industrial environments with legacy systems and heterogeneous data sources.

Model Interpretability: Interpreting and explaining the predictions of machine learning models used in predictive maintenance is crucial for gaining trust and acceptance from stakeholders. Interpretable models and visualization techniques are needed to understand the underlying factors driving equipment failures and maintenance decisions.

Deployment and Integration: Integrating predictive maintenance systems into existing workflows, maintenance practices, and decision-making processes requires careful planning and coordination. Seamless integration with asset management systems, enterprise resource planning (ERP) systems, and maintenance scheduling tools is essential for effective deployment.

Predictive maintenance is a transformative application of machine learning that enables organizations to proactively monitor and maintain critical assets, reduce downtime, and optimize maintenance costs. By leveraging techniques such as machine learning models, time-series analysis, anomaly detection, and survival analysis, predictive maintenance systems can predict equipment failures with high accuracy and enable timely maintenance interventions. In the next sections, we will explore other real-world examples of machine learning applications, further showcasing the breadth and impact of the field.

Recommendation Systems:

Recommendation systems leverage machine learning to personalize content or product recommendations based on user preferences and behavior. For example, streaming platforms like Netflix use collaborative filtering algorithms to suggest movies or TV shows similar to those a user has previously watched and enjoyed.

Recommendation systems are ubiquitous in today's digital landscape, influencing our choices in content consumption, product purchases, and more.

1. **Understanding Recommendation Systems:**

   Recommendation systems are algorithms that analyze user preferences, behavior, and historical interactions to provide personalized suggestions or recommendations. They aim to help users discover relevant content, products, or services based on their interests and preferences, enhancing user experience and engagement.

2. **Techniques and Algorithms:**

   Recommendation systems leverage various techniques and algorithms to generate personalized recommendations. Some common techniques and algorithms include:

   Collaborative Filtering: Collaborative filtering methods analyze user-item interactions (e.g., ratings, purchases) to identify similarities between users or items. Based on these similarities, recommendations are made to users who share similar tastes or preferences. Collaborative filtering can be further categorized into user-based and item-based approaches.

   Content-based Filtering: Content-based filtering methods analyze the features or attributes of items to recommend similar items to users based on their preferences. These methods rely on item metadata, such as text descriptions, tags, or attributes, to compute item similarities and make recommendations.

Matrix Factorization: Matrix factorization techniques decompose the user-item interaction matrix into lower-dimensional matrices to capture latent factors or features underlying user preferences and item characteristics. By learning latent representations of users and items, matrix factorization models can make personalized recommendations.

Deep Learning Models: Deep learning models, such as neural networks, can be used to learn complex patterns and relationships from user-item interactions and item attributes. Recurrent neural networks (RNNs), convolutional neural networks (CNNs), and transformer architectures have been applied to recommendation tasks, achieving state-of-the-art performance.

3. **Real-world Examples:**

Recommendation systems are widely deployed across various industries to personalize user experiences and drive engagement. Some notable real-world examples include:

E-commerce Platforms: Online retailers such as Amazon, Alibaba, and eBay use recommendation systems to suggest products to customers based on their browsing history, purchase history, and preferences. By analyzing user behavior and product attributes, these platforms can recommend relevant products, increase sales, and enhance customer satisfaction.

Streaming Services: Video streaming platforms such as Netflix, Hulu, and YouTube use recommendation systems to suggest movies, TV shows, and videos to users based on their viewing history, ratings, and preferences. By recommending personalized content, these platforms can increase user engagement and retention.

Social Media Platforms: Social media platforms such as Facebook, Instagram, and Twitter use recommendation systems to personalize users' feeds and suggest content, posts, or accounts to follow based on their interests, social connections, and engagement patterns. By showing relevant content, these platforms can increase user engagement and time spent on the platform.

Music Streaming Services: Music streaming platforms such as Spotify, Apple Music, and Pandora use recommendation systems to suggest songs, albums, and playlists to users based on their listening history, preferences, and behavior. By recommending personalized music, these platforms can enhance user satisfaction and retention.

4. **Challenges and Considerations:**

Despite their effectiveness, recommendation systems face several challenges and considerations, including:

Cold Start Problem: Recommendation systems may struggle to provide accurate recommendations for new users or items with limited historical data (cold start problem). Addressing the cold start problem requires techniques such as hybrid recommendation approaches, content-based recommendations, and active learning strategies.

Bias and Fairness: Recommendation systems may exhibit biases based on user demographics, preferences, or historical interactions, leading to unfair or discriminatory recommendations. Ensuring fairness and mitigating biases in recommendation systems requires careful data collection, algorithm design, and evaluation.

Privacy and Transparency: Recommendation systems often rely on user data and behavior to generate personalized recommendations, raising concerns about privacy and data protection. Providing transparency and control over data usage and recommendations is essential for building trust and maintaining user privacy.

Recommendation systems play a crucial role in personalizing user experiences and driving engagement across various digital platforms and services. By leveraging techniques such as collaborative filtering, content-based filtering, matrix factorization, and deep learning, recommendation systems can provide users with relevant and personalized recommendations, enhancing user satisfaction and driving business success. In the next sections, we will explore other real-world examples of machine learning applications, further illustrating the breadth and impact of the field.

Natural Language Processing (NLP):

NLP encompasses a range of machine learning techniques for understanding and processing human language. Sentiment analysis, for instance, involves analyzing text data to determine the sentiment or emotion expressed within it, enabling applications such as social media monitoring or customer feedback analysis.

Natural Language Processing (NLP) is a branch of artificial intelligence that focuses on the interaction between computers and humans through natural language. NLP enables machines to understand, interpret, and generate human language, facilitating a wide range of real-world applications.

1. **Understanding Natural Language Processing (NLP):**

   NLP encompasses a variety of tasks and techniques aimed at enabling machines to understand and process human language in a meaningful way. Some common NLP tasks include:

   Text Classification: Text classification involves categorizing text documents or sentences into predefined categories or classes. Examples include sentiment analysis, spam detection, topic classification, and language identification.

   Named Entity Recognition (NER): NER involves identifying and extracting named entities such as people, organizations, locations, dates, and numerical expressions from text documents. NER is used in applications such as information extraction, entity linking, and question answering.

   Machine Translation: Machine translation involves automatically translating text from one language to another. Examples include Google Translate, Microsoft Translator, and DeepL, which use statistical machine translation, neural machine translation, or transformer-based models to achieve accurate translations.

Question Answering: Question answering systems aim to automatically answer questions posed in natural language based on a given context or knowledge base. Examples include virtual assistants like Siri, Alexa, and Google Assistant, which can answer factual questions, provide information, and perform tasks based on user queries.

2. **Techniques and Algorithms:**

NLP leverages various techniques and algorithms to process and analyze natural language data. Some common techniques and algorithms include:

Tokenization: Tokenization involves splitting text into individual tokens or words. It is a fundamental preprocessing step in NLP tasks such as text classification, named entity recognition, and machine translation.

Word Embeddings: Word embeddings are dense, low-dimensional vector representations of words that capture semantic relationships and contextual information. Techniques such as Word2Vec, GloVe, and fastText are used to learn word embeddings from large text corpora.

Recurrent Neural Networks (RNNs): RNNs are a class of neural networks designed to process sequential data, making them well-suited for NLP tasks such as text generation, language modeling, and sequence labeling. Long Short-Term Memory (LSTM) and Gated Recurrent Unit (GRU) are popular variants of RNNs.

Transformer Architecture: Transformer architecture, introduced in the Transformer model, has revolutionized NLP by enabling efficient training of large-scale language models such as BERT, GPT, and T5. Transformers use self-attention mechanisms to capture long-range dependencies and contextual information in text sequences.

3. **Real-world Examples:**

NLP has numerous real-world applications across industries and domains. Some notable examples include:

Search Engines: Search engines like Google, Bing, and Yahoo use NLP techniques to understand user queries, analyze web pages, and retrieve relevant search results. NLP powers features such as auto-complete suggestions, semantic search, and natural language query processing.

Virtual Assistants: Virtual assistants such as Siri, Alexa, and Google Assistant leverage NLP to understand user commands, perform tasks, and provide information in natural language. NLP enables virtual assistants to recognize speech, extract intents, and generate appropriate responses.

Text Analytics: Text analytics platforms use NLP techniques to analyze large volumes of text data for insights and patterns. Industries such as finance, healthcare, and marketing use text analytics for sentiment analysis, trend detection, customer feedback analysis, and social media monitoring.

Chatbots: Chatbots are AI-powered conversational agents that interact with users in natural language. Chatbots use NLP techniques such as intent recognition, entity extraction, and dialogue management to understand user queries and provide relevant responses. They are used in customer service, e-commerce, and messaging platforms.

4. **Challenges and Considerations:**

Despite its advancements, NLP still faces several challenges and considerations, including:

Ambiguity and Context: Natural language is inherently ambiguous and context-dependent, making it challenging for machines to understand and interpret accurately. Resolving ambiguity and capturing context is crucial for achieving high accuracy in NLP tasks.

Data Quality and Bias: NLP models rely on large amounts of labeled data for training, which may contain biases and inaccuracies. Ensuring data quality, diversity, and fairness is essential for building robust and unbiased NLP systems.

Ethical and Privacy Concerns: NLP applications raise ethical and privacy concerns related to data privacy, consent, and algorithmic fairness. Addressing ethical considerations such as transparency, accountability, and bias mitigation is essential for responsible deployment of NLP systems.

Natural Language Processing (NLP) is a transformative field of machine learning that enables machines to understand, interpret, and generate human language. By leveraging techniques such as tokenization, word embeddings, recurrent neural networks, and transformer models, NLP powers a wide range of real-world applications across industries, including search engines, virtual assistants, text analytics, and chatbots. In the next sections, we will explore other real-world examples of machine learning applications, further illustrating the breadth and impact of the field.

Machine learning is a powerful tool that enables computers to learn from data and perform tasks that were once thought to be exclusive to human intelligence. With its diverse applications and transformative potential across industries, understanding the principles and techniques of machine learning is essential for anyone looking to harness the capabilities of artificial intelligence and drive innovation in the digital age.

Importance and Applications:

The significance of machine learning extends across virtually every industry and domain, driving innovation and transformation in areas such as healthcare, finance, marketing, transportation, and more. Its ability to automate tasks, optimize processes, and uncover hidden patterns has led to groundbreaking advancements and unprecedented opportunities for businesses and society as a whole.

In healthcare, machine learning is revolutionizing diagnostics, drug discovery, personalized medicine, and patient care. Financial institutions rely on machine learning algorithms for fraud detection, risk assessment, algorithmic trading, and customer segmentation. E-commerce platforms leverage machine learning for recommendation systems, customer profiling, and dynamic pricing. Autonomous vehicles use machine learning for navigation, object recognition, and decision-making in complex environments.

Machine learning (ML) is a powerful subset of artificial intelligence (AI) that enables computers to learn from data and make predictions or decisions without explicit programming. Its importance stems from its ability to analyze vast amounts of data, uncover hidden patterns, and generate insights that drive informed decision-making across various industries and domains.

1. **Significance of Machine Learning:** Machine learning plays a pivotal role in today's data-driven world, offering several key advantages:

Automation:

ML algorithms automate repetitive tasks and processes, reducing human intervention and freeing up valuable time for more strategic activities.

Machine learning (ML) is revolutionizing automation by enabling computers to learn from data and make decisions without explicit programming. This transformative technology has become increasingly important across various industries due to its ability to streamline processes, improve efficiency, and reduce human intervention

1. **Significance of Machine Learning in Automation:**

Machine learning plays a crucial role in automation by offering several key advantages:

Efficiency: ML algorithms automate repetitive tasks and processes, allowing organizations to accomplish tasks faster and more efficiently than manual methods.

Accuracy: ML models can analyze vast amounts of data and make predictions or decisions with high accuracy, reducing errors and improving overall quality.

Scalability: ML-based automation solutions can scale to handle large volumes of data and tasks, making them suitable for businesses of all sizes and industries.

Adaptability: ML algorithms can adapt and learn from new data, feedback, and experiences, making them well-suited for dynamic and evolving environments.

2. **Applications of Machine Learning in Automation:**

Machine learning finds extensive applications in automation across various industries and domains:

Manufacturing: In manufacturing, ML is used for predictive maintenance, quality control, process optimization, and supply chain management. ML algorithms analyze sensor data, equipment performance metrics, and production processes to predict equipment failures, detect defects, and optimize production schedules.

Customer Service: In customer service, ML powers chatbots, virtual assistants, sentiment analysis, and customer segmentation. ML models analyze customer interactions, feedback, and sentiment to automate customer support, provide personalized recommendations, and enhance customer satisfaction.

Finance: In finance, ML is used for fraud detection, risk assessment, algorithmic trading, credit scoring, and customer segmentation. ML models analyze transaction data to identify fraudulent activities and patterns, predict market trends, and optimize investment portfolios.

Healthcare: In healthcare, ML is used for medical imaging analysis, disease diagnosis, drug discovery, personalized treatment planning, and patient monitoring. ML algorithms can analyze medical images such as X-rays, MRIs, and CT scans to detect abnormalities and assist radiologists in diagnosis.

Transportation: In transportation, ML is used for route optimization, vehicle routing, traffic prediction, and autonomous vehicles. ML algorithms analyze traffic data, GPS data, and historical patterns to optimize routes, reduce congestion, and improve transportation efficiency.

E-commerce: In e-commerce, ML powers recommendation systems, personalized marketing, demand forecasting, and supply chain optimization. ML algorithms analyze user behavior, browsing history, and purchase patterns to recommend products, personalize marketing campaigns, and optimize inventory management.

Energy: In the energy sector, ML is used for predictive maintenance, energy consumption forecasting, fault detection, and smart grid optimization. ML algorithms analyze sensor data, weather forecasts, and historical patterns to predict equipment failures, optimize energy usage, and improve grid stability.

Machine learning is driving automation across industries by offering efficiency, accuracy, scalability, and adaptability. Its applications in manufacturing, customer service, finance, healthcare, transportation, e-commerce, energy, and other domains are transforming processes, improving productivity, and enhancing decision-making. As machine learning continues to advance, its role in automation is expected to expand, revolutionizing how organizations operate and innovate in the digital age.

Data-driven Insights:

ML enables organizations to extract valuable insights from large and complex datasets, leading to data-driven decision-making and strategic planning.

Machine learning (ML) is a powerful tool for deriving valuable insights from large and complex datasets, enabling data-driven decision-making across various industries. ML algorithms can uncover hidden patterns, trends, and relationships in data that humans may not easily discern, leading to informed strategic planning and actionable insights.

1. **Significance of Machine Learning in Data-driven Insights:**
   Machine learning plays a crucial role in generating data-driven insights by offering several key advantages:
   Scalability: ML algorithms can analyze large volumes of data quickly and efficiently, making them well-suited for handling big data and complex datasets.
   Accuracy: ML models can identify patterns and trends in data with high accuracy, reducing the risk of human error and bias in analysis.
   Prediction and Forecasting: ML algorithms can predict future trends, outcomes, and events based on historical data, enabling proactive decision-making and risk management.
   Automation: ML automates the process of data analysis, allowing organizations to extract insights faster and more efficiently than traditional methods.
2. **Applications of Machine Learning in Data-driven Insights:**

Machine learning finds extensive applications in generating data-driven insights across various industries and domains:

Marketing and Advertising: In marketing and advertising, ML is used for customer segmentation, personalized recommendations, churn prediction, and campaign optimization. ML algorithms analyze customer behavior, demographics, and interactions to target the right audience with relevant offers and messages.

Finance and Investment: In finance and investment, ML is used for risk assessment, fraud detection, algorithmic trading, and portfolio optimization. ML models analyze market data, trading patterns, and economic indicators to identify profitable investment opportunities and mitigate risks.

Healthcare and Medicine: In healthcare and medicine, ML is used for disease diagnosis, drug discovery, personalized treatment planning, and patient monitoring. ML algorithms analyze medical records, genomic data, and imaging studies to predict disease outcomes, identify drug targets, and tailor treatments to individual patients.

Supply Chain Management: In supply chain management, ML is used for demand forecasting, inventory optimization, route optimization, and predictive maintenance. ML algorithms analyze sales data, inventory levels, and shipping patterns to predict demand, optimize inventory levels, and streamline logistics operations.

Customer Service and Support: In customer service and support, ML is used for sentiment analysis, chatbots, virtual assistants, and customer feedback analysis. ML models analyze customer interactions, social media posts, and support tickets to understand sentiment, automate responses, and improve service quality.

Human Resources: In human resources, ML is used for talent acquisition, employee retention, performance evaluation, and workforce planning. ML algorithms analyze resumes, job postings, and employee data to identify top candidates, predict attrition, and optimize staffing levels.

Machine learning is instrumental in generating data-driven insights that drive informed decision-making and strategic planning across industries. Its scalability, accuracy, prediction capabilities, and automation make it a valuable tool for analyzing large and complex datasets to uncover valuable insights. From marketing and finance to healthcare and supply chain management, machine learning applications in generating data-driven insights are diverse and impactful. As organizations continue to leverage machine learning technologies, they can gain a competitive edge, improve efficiency, and drive innovation by harnessing the power of data-driven decision-making.Top of Form

Personalization:

ML algorithms personalize user experiences by analyzing user behavior, preferences, and interactions to deliver tailored recommendations, content, and services.

Machine learning (ML) plays a critical role in personalization by enabling businesses to tailor products, services, and experiences to individual preferences and characteristics. ML algorithms analyze user behavior, preferences, and interactions to deliver personalized recommendations, content, and services, enhancing user satisfaction and engagement.

1. **Significance of Machine Learning in Personalization:**

   Machine learning is essential for personalization due to several key reasons:

   Enhanced User Experience: Personalization improves user experience by delivering content, recommendations, and services that are relevant and valuable to individual users, increasing satisfaction and engagement.

   Increased Engagement: Personalized experiences lead to higher user engagement and retention as users are more likely to interact with content and services that are tailored to their interests and preferences.

   Improved Conversion Rates: Personalization can drive higher conversion rates by presenting users with relevant offers, recommendations, and promotions that resonate with their needs and preferences.

   Customer Loyalty: Personalization fosters customer loyalty and brand loyalty as users feel valued and understood when they receive personalized experiences, leading to repeat business and advocacy.

2. **Applications of Machine Learning in Personalization:**

Machine learning enables personalization across various industries and domains:

E-commerce: In e-commerce, ML is used for personalized product recommendations, personalized marketing campaigns, dynamic pricing, and personalized shopping experiences. ML algorithms analyze user browsing history, purchase behavior, and preferences to recommend products and offers tailored to individual users.

Streaming Services: In streaming services such as Netflix, Spotify, and Amazon Prime Video, ML powers personalized content recommendations, personalized playlists, and personalized content discovery. ML algorithms analyze user viewing or listening history, ratings, and preferences to recommend movies, TV shows, or music that match users' tastes.

Social Media: In social media platforms like Facebook, Instagram, and Twitter, ML is used for personalized content feeds, personalized ads, and personalized recommendations. ML algorithms analyze user interactions, interests, and social connections to curate personalized content and recommendations tailored to individual users.

Content Publishing: In content publishing platforms such as news websites, blogs, and content aggregators, ML enables personalized content recommendations, personalized news feeds, and personalized article suggestions. ML algorithms analyze user reading habits, interests, and engagement patterns to deliver relevant and engaging content to users.

Travel and Hospitality: In travel and hospitality, ML powers personalized travel recommendations, personalized hotel recommendations, and personalized travel itineraries. ML algorithms analyze user preferences, past bookings, and travel behavior to recommend destinations, accommodations, and activities that match users' preferences and interests.

Health and Fitness: In health and fitness apps and wearables, ML enables personalized workout recommendations, personalized nutrition plans, and personalized health insights. ML algorithms analyze user activity data, health metrics, and goals to provide personalized recommendations and guidance for achieving fitness and wellness goals.

Machine learning is instrumental in personalization, enabling businesses to deliver tailored experiences, recommendations, and services to individual users. From e-commerce and streaming services to social media and travel, machine learning applications in personalization are diverse and impactful, leading to enhanced user experiences, increased engagement, and improved business outcomes. As organizations continue to invest in personalization technologies, machine learning will play a central role in driving customer satisfaction, loyalty, and growth in the digital age.

Predictive Capabilities:

ML models can predict future outcomes, trends, and events based on historical data, enabling proactive decision-making and risk management.

Machine learning (ML) holds significant importance in predictive capabilities by enabling organizations to forecast future trends, outcomes, and events based on historical data and patterns. ML algorithms can analyze large datasets, identify relevant features, and make accurate predictions, helping businesses make proactive decisions, mitigate risks, and seize opportunities.

1. **Significance of Machine Learning in Predictive Capabilities:**

   Machine learning is crucial for predictive capabilities due to several key reasons:

   Proactive Decision-making: ML enables organizations to anticipate future trends, risks, and opportunities by analyzing historical data and making predictions, allowing them to make proactive decisions and take preemptive actions.

   Risk Mitigation: ML models can identify potential risks, threats, and anomalies by analyzing patterns and deviations in data, enabling organizations to implement risk mitigation strategies and safeguards.

   Opportunity Identification: ML algorithms can uncover

hidden patterns, correlations, and insights in data that humans may not easily discern, helping organizations identify new opportunities, market trends, and growth areas.

Resource Optimization: ML-based predictions can optimize resource allocation, planning, and scheduling by providing insights into demand forecasts, inventory levels, and production requirements, leading to cost savings and operational efficiency.

2. **Applications of Machine Learning in Predictive Capabilities:**

Machine learning enables predictive capabilities across various industries and domains:

Financial Forecasting: In finance, ML is used for stock price prediction, asset allocation, risk assessment, and credit scoring. ML algorithms analyze market data, economic indicators, and historical trends to forecast stock prices, identify investment opportunities, and assess credit risk.

Demand Forecasting: In retail and supply chain management, ML is used for demand forecasting, inventory optimization, and supply chain planning. ML models analyze sales data, customer behavior, and market trends to predict future demand, optimize inventory levels, and streamline logistics operations.

Healthcare Predictive Analytics: In healthcare, ML is used for disease prediction, patient monitoring, and treatment planning. ML algorithms analyze electronic health records, medical imaging data, and genomic data to predict disease outcomes, identify at-risk patients, and personalize treatment plans.

Predictive Maintenance: In manufacturing and asset-intensive industries, ML is used for predictive maintenance, equipment failure prediction, and condition monitoring. ML models analyze sensor data, equipment performance metrics, and maintenance logs to predict equipment failures, schedule maintenance proactively, and minimize downtime.

Customer Churn Prediction: In telecommunications, subscription-based services, and subscription-based businesses, ML is used for customer churn prediction and retention. ML algorithms analyze customer behavior, usage patterns, and demographics to identify customers at risk of churn and implement targeted retention strategies.

Weather Forecasting: In meteorology and climate science, ML is used for weather forecasting, extreme event prediction, and climate modeling. ML models analyze historical weather data, satellite imagery, and atmospheric variables to predict future weather patterns, severe storms, and climate trends.

Machine learning is instrumental in predictive capabilities, enabling organizations to forecast future trends, outcomes, and events based on historical data and patterns. From financial forecasting and demand forecasting to healthcare predictive analytics and customer churn prediction, machine learning applications in predictive capabilities are diverse and impactful, leading to proactive decision-making, risk mitigation, and resource optimization. As organizations continue to leverage machine learning technologies, predictive capabilities will play a central role in driving innovation, efficiency, and competitiveness in the digital age.

Optimization:

ML algorithms optimize processes, operations, and resources by identifying inefficiencies, bottlenecks, and opportunities for improvement.

Machine learning (ML) plays a crucial role in optimization by enabling organizations to improve processes, operations, and resource allocation through data-driven analysis and decision-making. ML algorithms can identify patterns, trends, and insights in data to optimize efficiency, productivity, and performance across various domains.

1. **Significance of Machine Learning in Optimization:**
   Machine learning is essential for optimization due to several key reasons:

Efficiency Improvement: ML algorithms can analyze large datasets and identify optimization opportunities, leading to improved efficiency, productivity, and resource utilization.

Cost Reduction: ML-based optimization can help organizations reduce costs by streamlining processes, minimizing waste, and optimizing resource allocation.

Performance Enhancement: ML algorithms can optimize systems, operations, and workflows to enhance performance, quality, and throughput.

Adaptability: ML-based optimization solutions can adapt and learn from new data and feedback, making them suitable for dynamic and evolving environments.

2. **Applications of Machine Learning in Optimization:**

Machine learning enables optimization across various industries and domains:

Supply Chain Optimization: In supply chain management, ML is used for demand forecasting, inventory optimization, and logistics planning. ML algorithms analyze historical sales data, market trends, and shipping patterns to predict demand, optimize inventory levels, and streamline distribution networks.

Production Process Optimization: In manufacturing, ML is used for process optimization, predictive maintenance, and quality control. ML models analyze sensor data, production metrics, and quality inspection results to identify inefficiencies, predict equipment failures, and improve product quality.

Resource Allocation: In project management and resource allocation, ML is used for resource optimization, scheduling, and task assignment. ML algorithms analyze project requirements, resource availability, and employee skills to optimize project timelines, allocate resources efficiently, and maximize productivity.

Energy Management: In energy management and sustainability, ML is used for energy optimization, demand response, and predictive maintenance. ML models analyze energy consumption data, weather forecasts, and building characteristics to optimize energy usage, reduce costs, and minimize environmental impact.

Financial Portfolio Optimization: In finance, ML is used for portfolio optimization, risk management, and algorithmic trading. ML algorithms analyze market data, economic indicators, and investment strategies to optimize portfolio allocations, mitigate risks, and maximize returns.

Customer Service Optimization: In customer service and support, ML is used for call routing, chatbot optimization, and sentiment analysis. ML models analyze customer interactions, feedback, and sentiment to optimize response times, automate routine inquiries, and improve service quality.

Machine learning is instrumental in optimization, enabling organizations to improve efficiency, reduce costs, and enhance performance across various domains. From supply chain optimization and production process optimization to resource allocation and energy management, machine learning applications in optimization are diverse and impactful, leading to tangible benefits such as cost savings, productivity gains, and competitive advantages. As organizations continue to leverage machine learning technologies, optimization will remain a key focus area for driving innovation and efficiency in the digital age.

2. Applications of Machine Learning:

Machine learning finds applications across a wide range of industries and domains, including:

Healthcare:

In healthcare, ML is used for medical imaging analysis, disease diagnosis, drug discovery, personalized treatment planning, and patient monitoring. ML algorithms can analyze medical images such as X-rays, MRIs, and CT scans to detect abnormalities and assist radiologists in diagnosis.

Machine learning (ML) has revolutionized healthcare by enabling the analysis of large volumes of medical data to improve diagnosis, treatment planning, patient monitoring, and operational efficiency. ML algorithms can uncover hidden patterns, predict disease outcomes, and personalize treatment strategies, leading to better patient outcomes and healthcare delivery.

1. **Disease Diagnosis and Medical Imaging:**

   Machine learning is used for disease diagnosis and medical imaging interpretation. ML algorithms analyze medical images such as X-rays, MRIs, CT scans, and mammograms to detect abnormalities, tumors, fractures, and other conditions. Deep learning models, such as convolutional neural networks (CNNs), have shown remarkable accuracy in image classification tasks, assisting radiologists in making faster and more accurate diagnoses.

2. **Predictive Analytics and Risk Stratification:**

   Machine learning enables predictive analytics and risk stratification to identify patients at risk of developing certain diseases or health complications. ML models analyze electronic health records (EHRs), medical histories, genetic data, and lifestyle factors to predict the likelihood of diseases such as diabetes, heart disease, cancer, and sepsis. Predictive analytics helps healthcare providers intervene early, implement preventive measures, and improve patient outcomes.

3. **Personalized Treatment Planning:**

   Machine learning is used to personalize treatment plans and interventions based on individual patient characteristics, genetic profiles, and treatment responses. ML algorithms analyze patient data, clinical guidelines, and medical literature to recommend personalized treatment options, dosage regimens, and therapeutic strategies. Personalized medicine aims to optimize treatment outcomes, minimize side effects, and improve patient adherence.

4. **Drug Discovery and Development:**

   Machine learning accelerates drug discovery and development by analyzing molecular structures, biological pathways, and drug interactions. ML algorithms predict the efficacy, safety, and toxicity of potential drug candidates, guiding researchers in selecting promising compounds for further experimentation and clinical trials. ML also facilitates drug repurposing, identifying existing drugs that may be effective for new indications or patient populations.

5. **Remote Patient Monitoring and Telemedicine:**

Machine learning enables remote patient monitoring and telemedicine, allowing healthcare providers to monitor patients' health status remotely and deliver virtual care. ML algorithms analyze continuous physiological data from wearable devices, sensors, and mobile apps to detect anomalies, track disease progression, and alert healthcare providers to potential emergencies. Telemedicine platforms use ML-powered chatbots and virtual assistants to provide medical advice, schedule appointments, and triage patient inquiries.

6. **Healthcare Operations and Resource Management:**

Machine learning optimizes healthcare operations and resource management by analyzing hospital operations, patient flow, and resource utilization. ML algorithms forecast patient admissions, allocate resources such as beds and staff, and optimize scheduling and staffing levels to improve efficiency and reduce wait times. Predictive maintenance models identify equipment failures and maintenance needs, minimizing downtime and ensuring the availability of critical medical devices.

Machine learning applications in healthcare are diverse and transformative, impacting every aspect of patient care, from diagnosis and treatment to monitoring and operations. As healthcare organizations continue to adopt ML technologies, they can improve clinical outcomes, enhance patient experiences, and optimize resource utilization, leading to a more efficient and effective healthcare system. Despite challenges such as data privacy, regulatory compliance, and algorithm transparency, machine learning holds tremendous promise for revolutionizing healthcare delivery and improving population health outcomes.

Finance:

In finance, ML is used for fraud detection, risk assessment, algorithmic trading, credit scoring, and customer segmentation. ML models analyze transaction data to identify fraudulent activities and patterns, predict market trends, and optimize investment portfolios.

Machine learning (ML) has significantly transformed the finance industry by enabling data-driven decision-making, risk management, fraud detection, and algorithmic trading. ML algorithms analyze large volumes of financial data to uncover patterns, predict market trends, and optimize investment strategies

1. **Algorithmic Trading and Quantitative Finance:**

   Machine learning is widely used in algorithmic trading and quantitative finance to develop trading strategies, forecast market movements, and optimize portfolio allocations. ML algorithms analyze historical market data, price trends, and trading signals to identify profitable trading opportunities and execute trades automatically. Reinforcement learning techniques are employed to develop trading agents that learn and adapt to changing market conditions.

2. **Risk Management and Credit Scoring:**

   Machine learning enables risk management and credit scoring to assess the creditworthiness of borrowers and manage financial risks. ML models analyze credit histories, financial transactions, and demographic data to predict the likelihood of default, assess credit risk, and determine appropriate loan terms. ML algorithms also identify fraudulent activities, detect anomalies, and mitigate operational risks in financial transactions.

3. **Fraud Detection and Anti-Money Laundering (AML):**

   Machine learning is used for fraud detection and anti-money

laundering (AML) to identify suspicious activities and prevent financial crimes. ML models analyze transaction data, user behavior, and transaction patterns to detect fraudulent transactions, money laundering activities, and suspicious behaviors. ML algorithms use anomaly detection, pattern recognition, and network analysis techniques to identify potential risks and mitigate fraud.

4. **Customer Relationship Management (CRM) and Personalized Services:**

Machine learning enhances customer relationship management (CRM) and enables personalized financial services. ML algorithms analyze customer data, transaction histories, and behavioral patterns to segment customers, identify preferences, and offer personalized recommendations, products, and services. ML-powered chatbots and virtual assistants provide personalized financial advice, assistance, and support to customers, enhancing customer engagement and satisfaction.

5. **Market Analysis and Sentiment Analysis:**

Machine learning facilitates market analysis and sentiment analysis to understand market dynamics and investor sentiment. ML algorithms analyze news articles, social media feeds, and market sentiment indicators to gauge investor sentiment, predict market trends, and assess market sentiment. Natural language processing (NLP) techniques are used to extract insights from unstructured text data and make informed investment decisions.

6. **Regulatory Compliance and Risk Assessment:**

Machine learning aids regulatory compliance and risk assessment by automating regulatory reporting, monitoring compliance with regulatory requirements, and assessing operational risks. ML models analyze regulatory texts, compliance documents, and transaction data to ensure adherence to regulations such as GDPR, Dodd-Frank, and Basel III.

ML algorithms also assess operational risks, identify compliance gaps, and recommend corrective actions to mitigate risks.

Machine learning applications in finance are diverse and impactful, driving innovation, efficiency, and risk management in the financial industry. From algorithmic trading and risk management to fraud detection and customer relationship management, machine learning technologies are transforming how financial institutions operate, make decisions, and interact with customers. As the volume and complexity of financial data continue to grow, machine learning will play an increasingly crucial role in shaping the future of finance and investment.

E-commerce:

In e-commerce, ML powers recommendation systems, personalized marketing, demand forecasting, and supply chain optimization. ML algorithms analyze user behavior, browsing history, and purchase patterns to recommend products, personalize marketing campaigns, and optimize inventory management.

Machine learning (ML) has revolutionized the e-commerce industry by enabling personalized recommendations, predictive analytics, fraud detection, and supply chain optimization. ML algorithms analyze vast amounts of customer data to deliver tailored shopping experiences, improve operational efficiency, and drive business growth.

1. **Personalized Product Recommendations:**

   Machine learning powers personalized product recommendations to enhance the shopping experience and increase sales. ML algorithms analyze user behavior, purchase history, and preferences to recommend products that are relevant and appealing to individual customers. Recommendation engines use techniques such as collaborative filtering, content-based filtering, and hybrid approaches to deliver personalized recommendations across various channels, including product pages, email, and advertisements.

2. **Predictive Analytics and Demand Forecasting:**

   Machine learning enables predictive analytics and demand forecasting to optimize inventory management and supply chain operations. ML models analyze historical sales data, website traffic, and market trends to predict future demand for products, anticipate stockouts, and optimize inventory levels. Predictive analytics helps e-commerce retailers improve product availability, reduce overstocking, and minimize fulfillment costs by aligning inventory with customer demand.

3. **Fraud Detection and Prevention:**

   Machine learning is used for fraud detection and prevention to combat fraudulent activities such as payment fraud, account takeover, and fake reviews. ML algorithms analyze transaction data, user behavior, and patterns of fraudulent activity to identify suspicious transactions, flag fraudulent accounts, and prevent unauthorized access. ML-powered fraud detection systems use anomaly detection, pattern recognition, and behavioral analysis techniques to detect and mitigate fraud in real time, protecting e-commerce businesses and customers from financial losses and reputational damage.

4. **Customer Segmentation and Targeted Marketing:**

   Machine learning facilitates customer segmentation and targeted marketing to improve customer acquisition and retention. ML algorithms analyze customer demographics, preferences, and purchase history to segment customers into groups based on their characteristics and behaviors. E-commerce retailers use customer segmentation to personalize marketing campaigns, tailor promotional offers, and optimize advertising spend by targeting the right audience with relevant messages and incentives.

5. **Dynamic Pricing and Revenue Optimization:**

   Machine learning enables dynamic pricing and revenue optimization to maximize profitability and competitiveness in e-commerce. ML algorithms analyze market dynamics, competitor pricing, and customer willingness to pay to set optimal prices for products and services. Dynamic pricing strategies adjust prices in real time based on factors such as demand, inventory levels, and customer behavior, helping e-commerce retailers capture more value and increase revenue.

6. Customer Service Automation:

Machine learning powers customer service automation to streamline support operations and enhance customer satisfaction. ML-powered chatbots and virtual assistants handle routine inquiries, provide product recommendations, and assist customers with order tracking, returns, and refunds. Natural language processing (NLP) techniques enable chatbots to understand and respond to customer queries in natural language, improving response times and efficiency in customer support.

Machine learning applications in e-commerce are diverse and transformative, driving personalized shopping experiences, operational efficiency, and business growth. From personalized product recommendations and demand forecasting to fraud detection and customer service automation, machine learning technologies are reshaping how e-commerce businesses operate, compete, and interact with customers. As e-commerce continues to evolve, machine learning will play an increasingly integral role in driving innovation and success in the digital marketplace.

Manufacturing:

In manufacturing, ML is used for predictive maintenance, quality control, process optimization, and supply chain management. ML models analyze sensor data, equipment performance metrics, and production processes to predict equipment failures, detect defects, and optimize production schedules.

Machine learning (ML) has brought significant advancements to the manufacturing industry by improving efficiency, quality control, predictive maintenance, and supply chain management. ML algorithms analyze large volumes of production data to optimize processes, detect anomalies, and predict equipment failures, leading to increased productivity and reduced costs.

1. **Predictive Maintenance:**

   Machine learning enables predictive maintenance by analyzing sensor data, equipment performance metrics, and maintenance logs to predict equipment failures before they occur. ML algorithms use historical data to identify patterns and anomalies indicative of impending failures, enabling proactive maintenance activities to be scheduled, minimizing unplanned downtime, and reducing maintenance costs.

2. **Quality Control and Defect Detection:**

   Machine learning improves quality control and defect detection in manufacturing processes by analyzing visual inspection data, sensor readings, and process parameters. ML algorithms can detect defects, anomalies, and deviations from quality standards in real-time, enabling immediate corrective actions to be taken to prevent defective products from reaching customers. Computer vision techniques are used to analyze images and identify defects such as scratches, dents, and misalignments on manufactured parts.

3. **Process Optimization and Yield Improvement:**

   Machine learning optimizes manufacturing processes and improves yield by analyzing production data, sensor readings, and historical performance metrics. ML algorithms identify optimal process parameters, recipe settings, and operating conditions to maximize throughput, minimize waste, and improve product quality. Process optimization techniques such as reinforcement learning and genetic algorithms are used to iteratively improve process efficiency and performance.

4. **Supply Chain Management:**

   Machine learning enhances supply chain management in manufacturing by optimizing inventory levels, demand forecasting, and logistics operations. ML algorithms analyze sales data, market trends, and supplier performance to predict demand, optimize inventory levels, and improve delivery scheduling. Supply chain optimization techniques such as inventory optimization, network optimization, and route optimization are used to reduce costs, improve efficiency, and enhance responsiveness in the supply chain.

5. **Energy Management and Sustainability:**

Machine learning optimizes energy management and promotes sustainability in manufacturing by analyzing energy consumption data, production schedules, and environmental factors. ML algorithms identify energy-saving opportunities, optimize energy usage, and reduce carbon emissions by optimizing production schedules, adjusting equipment settings, and implementing energy-efficient practices. Energy management systems powered by ML help manufacturers reduce energy costs, comply with environmental regulations, and minimize their carbon footprint.

6. **Human-Machine Collaboration:**

Machine learning enables human-machine collaboration in manufacturing by augmenting human capabilities with intelligent automation and robotics. ML algorithms analyze sensor data and human-machine interaction patterns to optimize task allocation, improve safety, and enhance productivity on the factory floor. Collaborative robots, or cobots, equipped with ML capabilities, work alongside human operators to perform complex tasks, handle repetitive tasks, and assist with assembly, welding, and material handling operations.

Machine learning applications in manufacturing are diverse and transformative, driving efficiency, quality, and sustainability in production processes. From predictive maintenance and quality control to supply chain management and energy optimization, machine learning technologies are reshaping how manufacturers operate, compete, and innovate in the digital age. As manufacturing continues to evolve, machine learning will play an increasingly integral role in driving productivity, competitiveness, and sustainability in the manufacturing industry.

Transportation:

In transportation, ML is used for route optimization, vehicle routing, traffic prediction, and autonomous vehicles. ML algorithms analyze traffic data, GPS data, and historical patterns to optimize routes, reduce congestion, and improve transportation efficiency.

Machine learning (ML) has revolutionized the transportation industry by enabling advancements in autonomous vehicles, route optimization, traffic prediction, and fleet management. ML algorithms analyze vast amounts of transportation data to improve safety, efficiency, and sustainability in various modes of transportation.

1. **Autonomous Vehicles:**

    Machine learning powers autonomous vehicles by enabling them to perceive their environment, make decisions, and navigate safely without human intervention. ML algorithms process sensor data from cameras, LiDAR, radar, and GPS to detect obstacles, recognize traffic signs, and plan optimal routes. Deep learning models, such as convolutional neural networks (CNNs) and recurrent neural networks (RNNs), learn from large datasets of labeled images and sensor data to improve object recognition and decision-making capabilities in autonomous vehicles.

2. **Route Optimization and Navigation:**

    Machine learning optimizes route planning and navigation in transportation systems by analyzing traffic patterns, road conditions, and historical data. ML algorithms use real-time traffic data, GPS coordinates, and user preferences to calculate the fastest, most fuel-efficient, or least congested routes for vehicles, cyclists, and pedestrians. Route optimization techniques such as reinforcement learning and genetic algorithms adaptively adjust routes based on changing traffic conditions and user feedback, improving overall efficiency and reducing travel time.

3. **Traffic Prediction and Congestion Management:**

Machine learning predicts traffic congestion and manages traffic flow by analyzing historical traffic data, weather conditions, and event schedules. ML models forecast traffic patterns, congestion hotspots, and travel times to inform route planning, public transit schedules, and congestion mitigation strategies. Predictive analytics enables transportation agencies and ride-sharing services to anticipate demand, optimize service levels, and alleviate congestion by rerouting traffic and adjusting transportation services dynamically.

4. **Public Transit Optimization:**

Machine learning optimizes public transit operations and improves service quality by analyzing ridership data, scheduling constraints, and service reliability metrics. ML algorithms optimize transit schedules, allocate resources, and optimize service frequencies to maximize passenger satisfaction and minimize waiting times. Real-time data analytics enable transit agencies to monitor service performance, identify service disruptions, and respond to passenger feedback promptly, enhancing the overall transit experience.

5. **Freight Logistics and Supply Chain Management:**

Machine learning enhances freight logistics and supply chain management by optimizing cargo routing, delivery scheduling, and warehouse operations. ML algorithms analyze shipping data, inventory levels, and demand forecasts to optimize freight routes, minimize transportation costs, and improve delivery reliability. Predictive analytics enables logistics companies to anticipate demand fluctuations, optimize inventory levels, and streamline distribution networks, ensuring timely delivery and customer satisfaction.

6. **Vehicle Maintenance and Fleet Management:**

Machine learning improves vehicle maintenance and fleet management by predicting equipment failures, optimizing maintenance schedules, and reducing downtime. ML algorithms analyze sensor data, maintenance records, and historical performance metrics to identify potential issues, schedule maintenance proactively, and optimize fleet operations. Predictive maintenance techniques such as anomaly detection and failure prediction enable transportation companies to reduce maintenance costs, extend equipment lifespan, and improve fleet reliability.

Machine learning applications in transportation are diverse and transformative, driving advancements in autonomous vehicles, route optimization, traffic prediction, and logistics management. From improving safety and efficiency in autonomous vehicles to optimizing public transit operations and freight logistics, machine learning technologies are reshaping how people and goods move in the modern world. As transportation continues to evolve, machine learning will play an increasingly integral role in shaping the future of mobility, connectivity, and sustainability in transportation systems.

Customer Service:

In customer service, ML powers chatbots, virtual assistants, sentiment analysis, and customer segmentation. ML models analyze customer interactions, feedback, and sentiment to automate customer support, provide personalized recommendations, and enhance customer satisfaction.

Machine learning (ML) has revolutionized customer service by enabling personalized interactions, automated support, sentiment analysis, and predictive customer analytics. ML algorithms analyze large volumes of customer data to improve response times, enhance satisfaction, and optimize service delivery across various channels.

1. **Automated Customer Support:**

Machine learning powers automated customer support systems, such as chatbots and virtual assistants, to handle routine inquiries, provide instant responses, and assist customers 24/7. ML algorithms use natural language processing (NLP) techniques to understand and generate human-like responses to customer queries, reducing wait times and improving efficiency in customer service.

2. **Personalized Recommendations and Offers:**

Machine learning enables personalized recommendations and offers to enhance the customer experience and increase engagement. ML algorithms analyze customer behavior, preferences, and purchase history to recommend products, services, and promotions tailored to individual preferences. Personalized recommendations improve conversion rates, drive repeat purchases, and foster customer loyalty by delivering relevant and timely offers.

3. **Sentiment Analysis and Customer Feedback:**

Machine learning performs sentiment analysis and customer feedback analysis to understand customer satisfaction, identify issues, and improve service quality. ML algorithms analyze customer reviews, social media posts, and survey responses to extract insights, identify trends, and measure sentiment. Sentiment analysis helps businesses identify areas for improvement, address customer concerns, and enhance the overall customer experience.

4. **Predictive Customer Analytics:**

Machine learning enables predictive customer analytics to anticipate customer needs, preferences, and behavior. ML algorithms analyze customer data, demographic information, and interaction history to predict future purchase intent, churn risk, and customer lifetime value. Predictive analytics enables businesses to personalize marketing campaigns, tailor product offerings, and proactively address customer needs, increasing customer satisfaction and retention.

5. **Voice Recognition and Speech-to-Text:**

   Machine learning powers voice recognition and speech-to-text technologies to improve customer interactions and accessibility. ML algorithms convert spoken language into text, enabling customers to interact with automated systems using voice commands. Voice recognition technologies enable hands-free interactions, improve accessibility for users with disabilities, and enhance the usability of customer service applications.

6. **Omnichannel Support and Integration:**

Machine learning facilitates omnichannel support and integration by providing a seamless customer experience across multiple channels and touchpoints. ML algorithms analyze customer interactions, preferences, and context to personalize interactions and maintain continuity across channels such as phone, email, chat, and social media. Omnichannel support ensures consistency, convenience, and efficiency in customer service interactions, improving customer satisfaction and loyalty.

Machine learning applications in customer service are diverse and transformative, driving efficiency, personalization, and customer satisfaction. From automated support and personalized recommendations to sentiment analysis and predictive analytics, machine learning technologies are reshaping how businesses interact with and serve their customers. As customer expectations continue to evolve, machine learning will play an increasingly integral role in delivering exceptional customer experiences and driving business success.

Natural Language Processing (NLP):

In NLP, ML is used for text classification, sentiment analysis, machine translation, and question answering. ML models analyze text data from sources such as social media, news articles, and customer reviews to extract insights, understand user intent, and generate responses.

Natural Language Processing (NLP) is a branch of artificial intelligence that focuses on the interaction between computers and humans through natural language. Machine learning (ML) plays a central role in NLP by enabling computers to understand, interpret, and generate human language.

1. **Text Classification and Sentiment Analysis:**

   Machine learning is used for text classification and sentiment analysis to categorize text documents and determine the sentiment expressed within them. ML algorithms analyze text data and assign labels or categories to classify documents into predefined categories such as spam detection, topic classification, or sentiment analysis (positive, negative, or neutral). Sentiment analysis techniques enable businesses to understand customer opinions, assess brand sentiment, and monitor social media discussions.

2. **Named Entity Recognition (NER) and Information Extraction:**

   Machine learning enables Named Entity Recognition (NER) and information extraction to identify and extract named entities such as names, organizations, locations, and dates from text documents. ML algorithms use pattern recognition and contextual cues to recognize and classify named entities in unstructured text data. NER and information extraction techniques are used in applications such as entity linking, knowledge extraction, and document summarization.

3. **Language Translation and Multilingual Processing:**

   Machine learning powers language translation and multilingual processing to facilitate communication across different languages and cultures. ML algorithms analyze parallel corpora and learn translation mappings between languages, enabling automatic translation of text from one language to another. Neural machine translation (NMT) models, based on deep learning architectures, achieve state-of-the-art performance in language translation tasks and support multilingual processing in applications such as cross-lingual information retrieval and localization.

4. **Text Generation and Natural Language Generation (NLG):**

Machine learning enables text generation and natural language generation (NLG) to generate human-like text based on input data or prompts. ML algorithms, such as recurrent neural networks (RNNs) and transformers, learn to generate coherent and contextually relevant text by modeling the probability distribution of words or characters in a language. Text generation techniques are used in applications such as chatbots, virtual assistants, and content generation for personalized recommendations or summaries.

5. **Question Answering and Conversational AI:**

Machine learning facilitates question answering and conversational AI to enable computers to understand and respond to natural language queries and engage in human-like conversations. ML algorithms analyze question-answer pairs and learn to generate accurate responses to user queries by leveraging knowledge graphs, semantic parsing, and contextual understanding. Question answering systems and conversational agents powered by machine learning enable interactive dialogue and information retrieval in applications such as virtual assistants, customer support chatbots, and voice-enabled devices.

6. **Text Summarization and Document Understanding:**

Machine learning enables text summarization and document understanding to distill large volumes of text into concise summaries or extract key information from documents. ML algorithms use extractive or abstractive summarization techniques to identify important sentences or phrases in a document and generate a summary that captures the main points. Text summarization and document understanding techniques support tasks such as document clustering, topic modeling, and information retrieval in applications such as news aggregation, document management, and literature review.

Machine learning applications in natural language processing (NLP) are diverse and transformative, enabling computers to understand, interpret, and generate human language with increasing accuracy and fluency. From text classification and sentiment analysis to language translation and conversational AI, machine learning technologies are reshaping how we interact with and process natural language data. As NLP continues to advance, machine learning will play an increasingly integral role in powering intelligent systems that understand and communicate with humans in natural language.

Image and Video Analysis:

In image and video analysis, ML is used for object detection, image classification, facial recognition, and video summarization. ML algorithms analyze visual data from sources such as surveillance cameras, satellites, and medical imaging devices to identify objects, recognize faces, and extract useful information.

Machine learning (ML) has revolutionized image and video analysis by enabling computers to understand, interpret, and extract meaningful information from visual data. ML algorithms analyze images and videos to perform tasks such as object detection, classification, segmentation, and recognition, leading to advancements in various fields

1. **Object Detection and Recognition:**

   Machine learning enables object detection and recognition to identify and localize objects within images or videos. ML algorithms analyze visual data and detect objects of interest by drawing bounding boxes around them. Object detection techniques, such as convolutional neural networks (CNNs) and region-based methods, achieve high accuracy in recognizing objects in real-world scenes. Object recognition applications include autonomous vehicles, surveillance systems, and augmented reality.

2. **Image Classification and Labeling:**

   Machine learning powers image classification and labeling to categorize images into predefined classes or categories. ML algorithms analyze visual features and learn to distinguish between different objects, scenes, or patterns present in images. Image classification models, such as deep convolutional neural networks (CNNs), achieve state-of-the-art performance in tasks such as image recognition, content moderation, and medical imaging diagnosis.

3. **Image Segmentation and Semantic Understanding:**

   Machine learning enables image segmentation and semantic understanding to partition images into meaningful regions and infer the semantic context of visual scenes. ML algorithms analyze pixel-level features and classify each pixel into semantic categories such as objects, backgrounds, or regions of interest. Image segmentation techniques, such as convolutional neural networks (CNNs) and fully convolutional networks (FCNs), are used in applications such as medical image analysis, autonomous driving, and satellite imagery interpretation.

4. **Facial Recognition and Biometric Identification:**

   Machine learning powers facial recognition and biometric identification to recognize and authenticate individuals based on facial features or biometric characteristics. ML algorithms analyze facial images and extract distinctive features, such as facial landmarks or biometric patterns, to match faces against known identities or verify identity claims. Facial recognition applications include access control systems, surveillance cameras, and identity verification platforms.

5. **Video Surveillance and Anomaly Detection:**

   Machine learning enables video surveillance and anomaly detection to monitor and analyze video streams in real-time for abnormal activities or events. ML algorithms analyze temporal patterns and detect anomalies, such as intruders, accidents, or suspicious behavior, in video data. Video surveillance systems powered by machine learning provide enhanced security and situational awareness in applications such as smart cities, transportation hubs, and critical infrastructure protection.

6. **Action Recognition and Gesture Detection:**

Machine learning powers action recognition and gesture detection to recognize and interpret human actions or gestures from video sequences. ML algorithms analyze motion patterns and spatial-temporal features to classify actions or gestures performed by individuals in videos. Action recognition applications include human-computer interaction, sign language recognition, and sports analytics for analyzing player movements and tactics.

Machine learning applications in image and video analysis are diverse and transformative, enabling computers to understand and interpret visual data with human-like accuracy and efficiency. From object detection and image classification to facial recognition and video surveillance, machine learning technologies are reshaping how we analyze and extract information from images and videos. As image and video analysis continue to advance, machine learning will play an increasingly integral role in powering intelligent systems that perceive and interpret visual information in the digital age.

Machine learning is a transformative technology with significant importance and diverse applications across industries and domains. By leveraging its automation capabilities, data-driven insights, predictive capabilities, and optimization algorithms, organizations can drive innovation, improve efficiency, and gain a competitive edge in today's dynamic business landscape. As ML continues to advance, its impact on society and the economy is expected to grow, shaping the future of industries, businesses, and everyday life.

Conclusion:

From speech recognition and natural language processing to computer vision and robotics, the applications of machine learning are vast and diverse, with new breakthroughs emerging regularly. As such, understanding the principles and techniques of machine learning is essential for anyone looking to harness its transformative potential and drive innovation in their respective fields.

Chapter 2: Foundations of Programming Languages

Foundations of Programming Languages refers to the fundamental principles and concepts underlying the design, implementation, and usage of programming languages. Understanding these foundational concepts is crucial for programmers and software developers to write efficient, reliable, and maintainable code.

1. **Syntax and Semantics:**

   Syntax refers to the rules that define the structure and composition of valid program statements, while semantics defines the meaning and behavior of those statements. For example, in the Python programming language, the syntax for a conditional statement (if-else) is:

   if condition:

   # code block executed if condition is true

   else:

   # code block executed if condition is false

   Here, the syntax dictates the structure of the if-else statement. The semantics define that the code block following the **if** statement is executed if the condition evaluates to **True**, otherwise, the code block following the **else** statement is executed.

2. **Data Types and Variables:**

   Programming languages support various data types such as

integers, floats, strings, and booleans, which define the type of data that can be stored and manipulated. Variables are used to store and manipulate data within a program. For example, in Java:

int num = 10; // declaring an integer variable

double pi = 3.14; // declaring a double variable

String message = "Hello, world!"; // declaring a string variable

boolean isTrue = true; // declaring a boolean variable

Here, **num**, **pi**, **message**, and **isTrue** are variables of different data types storing integer, double, string, and boolean values respectively.

3. **Control Structures:**

Control structures determine the flow of execution within a program based on certain conditions or loops. Examples include if statements, loops (such as for, while), and switch statements. For instance, in C++:

```
int x = 5;
if (x > 0) {
// code block executed if x is greater than 0
}
else {
// code block executed if x is less than or equal to 0
}
```

Here, the if statement controls the flow of execution based on whether the condition **x > 0** is true or false.

4. **Functions and Procedures:**

Functions and procedures encapsulate a sequence of statements that perform a specific task. Functions return a value, while procedures do not. For example, in Python:

```
def add(x, y):
return x + y
result = add(3, 5)
print(result) # Output: 8
```

Here, the **add** function takes two parameters **x** and **y**, adds them together, and returns the result.

5. **Abstraction and Encapsulation:**

Abstraction involves hiding unnecessary details and exposing only essential features to the user, making programs easier to understand and maintain. Encapsulation involves bundling data and functions that operate on that data into a single unit (class in object-oriented programming). For instance, in Java:

```
class Rectangle {
private int length;
private int width;
public Rectangle(int length, int width) {
this.length = length;
this.width = width;
}
public int calculateArea() {
return length * width;
}
}
```

Here, the **Rectangle** class encapsulates data (length and width) and functions (calculateArea) that operate on that data, providing a clear abstraction of a geometric rectangle.

Conclusion

Understanding the foundations of programming languages is essential for mastering programming concepts, writing efficient code, and designing robust software systems. By grasping syntax, semantics, data types, control structures, functions, abstraction, and encapsulation, programmers can develop well-structured, maintainable, and scalable software solutions across various domains and platforms.

Overview of Programming Paradigms:

Programming paradigms represent fundamental styles or approaches to programming, each with its own set of principles, concepts, and techniques. Understanding different programming paradigms is essential for programmers to select the most appropriate language and design patterns for solving specific problems efficiently.

1. Imperative Programming Paradigm:

Imperative programming is one of the fundamental programming paradigms, focusing on describing computation as a sequence of statements that change the program's state. In imperative programming, programs consist of instructions that explicitly specify how to perform tasks and manipulate data. This paradigm is characterized by mutable state, control structures, and procedures or subroutines. Here, we delve into the key aspects of the imperative programming paradigm with examples to illustrate its characteristics and applications.

1. **Mutable State:**

   In imperative programming, variables are mutable, meaning their values can be changed during program execution. Programs maintain state through the manipulation of variables, which store data that may be modified over time. This mutable state facilitates the sequential execution of instructions and enables programs to react dynamically to input and produce output.

   Example (in Python):

   ```python
   # Assigning values to variables and modifying their values
   x = 5
   y = 3
   result = x + y # result = 8
   x = 10 # changing the value of x
   result = x + y # result = 13
   ```

2. **Control Structures:**

Imperative programming relies on control structures such as conditionals (if-else statements), loops (for, while), and branching (goto statements) to control the flow of execution within a program. These control structures dictate the order in which statements are executed based on specific conditions or iterations.

Example (in C):

```c
// Using if-else statements to control the flow of execution
int x = 5;
if (x > 0) {
printf("x is positive\n");
} else {
printf("x is non-positive\n");
}
```

3. **Procedures or Subroutines:**

Imperative programming emphasizes the use of procedures or subroutines to organize code into reusable units that perform specific tasks. Procedures encapsulate a sequence of statements or actions and can accept parameters and return values. This modular approach promotes code reuse, readability, and maintainability.

Example (in Java):

```java
// Defining a method (procedure) to calculate the factorial of a number
public static int factorial(int n) {
int result = 1;
for (int i = 1; i <= n; i++) {
result *= i;
}
return result;
}
```

4. **Stateful Programming:**

Imperative programming is inherently stateful, meaning that the program's behavior depends on the current state of variables and memory. State changes occur through assignments, modifications, and updates to mutable variables, enabling programs to maintain and manipulate state over time.

Example (in JavaScript):

```javascript
// Modifying the state of variables using assignments
let count = 0;
function increment() {
count += 1;
}
increment(); // count = 1
increment(); // count = 2
```

5. **Example Application - Mathematical Operations:**

Imperative programming is well-suited for applications that involve sequential computation, control flow, and state manipulation. For example, mathematical operations, algorithms, and procedural tasks can be efficiently implemented using imperative programming languages such as C, Java, and Python.

The imperative programming paradigm provides a structured approach to building software systems by emphasizing mutable state, control structures, and procedures. By understanding and applying imperative programming concepts, programmers can develop efficient, readable, and maintainable code for a wide range of applications, from mathematical computations to system-level programming. However, it's important to recognize that imperative programming may lead to issues such as side effects, mutable state management, and spaghetti code if not used judiciously.

2. Functional Programming Paradigm:

Functional programming is a programming paradigm that treats computation as the evaluation of mathematical functions and avoids changing-state and mutable data. It emphasizes the use of functions as first-class citizens, immutability, and higher-order functions. In functional programming, programs are composed of pure functions that produce outputs solely based on their inputs, without side effects. Here, we delve into the key aspects of the functional programming paradigm with examples to illustrate its characteristics and applications.

1. **Pure Functions:**

    In functional programming, pure functions are functions that always return the same output for a given input and have no side effects. They do not rely on or modify external state, making them deterministic and easy to reason about. Pure functions facilitate modularity, reusability, and parallelism in functional programs.

    Example (in Haskell):

    ```haskell
    -- Pure function to calculate the factorial of a number
    factorial :: Integer -> Integer
    factorial 0 = 1
    factorial n = n * factorial (n - 1)
    ```

2. **Immutability:**

    Functional programming promotes immutability, meaning that data structures and variables are immutable once created and cannot be modified. Instead of mutating existing data, functional programs create new data structures through transformations and transformations, preserving the original data's integrity.

    Example (in Scala):

    ```scala
    // Immutable list operations in functional programming
    val numbers = List(1, 2, 3, 4, 5)
    val squaredNumbers = numbers.map(x => x * x) // Create a new
    list with squared numbers
    ```

3. **Higher-Order Functions:**

    Functional programming treats functions as first-class citizens, allowing functions to be passed as arguments to other functions, returned as values from other functions, and stored in data structures. Higher-order functions enable abstraction, composition, and modularity in functional programs.

Example (in JavaScript):

```javascript
// Higher-order function to apply a function to each element of
an array
function map(array, fn) {
let result = [];
for (let i = 0; i < array.length; i++) {
result.push(fn(array[i]));
}
return result;
}
let numbers = [1, 2, 3, 4, 5];
let squaredNumbers = map(numbers, x => x * x);
```

4. **Referential Transparency:**

Functional programming emphasizes referential transparency, where expressions can be replaced with their values without changing the program's behavior. This property simplifies reasoning about program behavior, enables optimization, and facilitates equational reasoning.

Example (in Haskell):

```haskell
-- Referentially transparent function to calculate the sum of
squares
sumOfSquares :: Integer -> Integer -> Integer
sumOfSquares x y = square x + square y
where square n = n * n
```

5. **Example Application - List Processing:**

Functional programming is well-suited for applications that involve list processing, transformations, and data manipulation. Functional programming languages such as Haskell, Lisp, and Scala are commonly used for tasks such as data analysis, data processing pipelines, and algorithmic problem-solving.

The functional programming paradigm provides a concise, declarative, and elegant approach to building software systems by emphasizing pure functions, immutability, and higher-order functions. By understanding and applying functional programming concepts, programmers can develop scalable, parallelizable, and maintainable code for a wide range of applications, from mathematical computations to data processing pipelines. However, it's important to recognize that functional programming may require a shift in mindset for programmers accustomed to imperative programming paradigms and mutable state management.

3. Object-Oriented Programming (OOP) Paradigm:

Object-Oriented Programming (OOP) is a programming paradigm based on the concept of "objects," which encapsulate data and behavior. It emphasizes modularity, encapsulation, inheritance, and polymorphism. In OOP, programs are organized as a collection of objects that interact with each other to perform tasks. Here, we delve into the key aspects of the Object-Oriented Programming paradigm with examples to illustrate its characteristics and applications.

1. **Classes and Objects:**

    In Object-Oriented Programming, classes are blueprints or templates that define the properties (attributes) and behaviors (methods) of objects. Objects are instances of classes, representing concrete entities with specific data and behavior. Classes encapsulate data and behavior into a single unit, promoting code reuse and modularity.

    Example (in Java):

```java
// Defining a class representing a Car
public class Car {
// Attributes
private String brand;
private String model;
private int year;
```

```
// Constructor
public Car(String brand, String model, int year) {
this.brand = brand;
this.model = model;
this.year = year;
}
// Method to display car information
public void displayInfo() {
System.out.println("Brand: " + brand);
System.out.println("Model: " + model);
System.out.println("Year: " + year);
}
}
// Creating objects of the Car class
Car car1 = new Car("Toyota", "Camry", 2020);
Car car2 = new Car("Honda", "Civic", 2019);
// Accessing object methods
car1.displayInfo();
car2.displayInfo();
```

2. **Encapsulation:**

Encapsulation is the principle of bundling data (attributes) and methods (behavior) within a class and restricting access to the internal state of objects. It hides the implementation details of objects and exposes only essential interfaces, enhancing data security and code maintainability.

Example (in C++):

```
// Encapsulation in C++ using classes
#include <iostream>
using namespace std;
// Class representing a Rectangle
class Rectangle {
private:
int length;
int width;
```

```cpp
public:
// Constructor
Rectangle(int l, int w) {
length = l;
width = w;
}
// Method to calculate area
int calculateArea() {
return length * width;
}
};
int main() {
Rectangle rect(5, 4);
cout << "Area: " << rect.calculateArea() << endl;
return 0;
}
```

3. **Inheritance:**

Inheritance is the mechanism by which one class (subclass or derived class) inherits properties and behaviors from another class (superclass or base class). It promotes code reuse and allows for the creation of hierarchical relationships between classes.

Example (in Python):

```python
# Inheritance in Python
class Animal:
def speak(self):
print("Animal speaks")
class Dog(Animal):
def bark(self):
print("Dog barks")
# Creating objects
animal = Animal()
dog = Dog()
# Calling methods
animal.speak() # Output: Animal speaks
```

```
dog.speak() # Output: Animal speaks
dog.bark() # Output: Dog barks
```

4. **Polymorphism:**

Polymorphism allows objects of different classes to be treated as objects of a common superclass. It enables methods to be overridden in subclasses, providing different implementations based on the object's type. Polymorphism promotes flexibility and extensibility in object-oriented designs.

Example (in Java):

```java
// Polymorphism in Java
class Animal {
public void sound() {
System.out.println("Animal makes a sound");
}
}
class Dog extends Animal {
@Override
public void sound() {
System.out.println("Dog barks");
}
}
class Cat extends Animal {
@Override
public void sound() {
System.out.println("Cat meows");
}
}
// Creating objects
Animal animal1 = new Dog();
Animal animal2 = new Cat();
// Calling methods
animal1.sound(); // Output: Dog barks
animal2.sound(); // Output: Cat meows
```

The Object-Oriented Programming paradigm provides a powerful and flexible approach to building software systems by emphasizing encapsulation, inheritance, polymorphism, and modularity. By understanding and applying OOP concepts, programmers can develop modular, reusable, and maintainable code for a wide range of applications, from software development to system design. However, it's important to recognize that OOP may require a shift in mindset for programmers accustomed to procedural programming paradigms and imperative programming styles.

4. Declarative Programming Paradigm:

Declarative programming is a programming paradigm that emphasizes expressing the logic of a computation without specifying the control flow explicitly. Instead of focusing on how to achieve a result, declarative programming focuses on describing what should be accomplished. This paradigm often relies on high-level abstractions and domain-specific languages to express computation concisely and efficiently.

1. **Declarative vs. Imperative:**

   Declarative programming differs from imperative programming in that it focuses on describing the problem domain and desired outcomes rather than specifying step-by-step instructions for achieving those outcomes. While imperative programming describes how to perform computations using explicit control flow statements, declarative programming abstracts away control flow and emphasizes the logic of the computation.

2. **SQL (Structured Query Language):**

   SQL is a prime example of declarative programming used for querying and manipulating relational databases. Instead of specifying how to retrieve data from a database, SQL queries express what data is needed. Users describe the desired data set by specifying conditions, projections, and joins, and the database management system (DBMS) determines the most efficient way to execute the query.

Example (in SQL):

```
-- Declarative SQL query to retrieve employee names and salaries from a database
SELECT name, salary FROM employees WHERE department = 'Engineering';
```

3. **Functional Programming Languages:**

   Functional programming languages, such as Haskell and Erlang, often exhibit declarative characteristics by emphasizing function composition, immutability, and higher-order functions. Functional programming languages enable developers to express computations as a series of function applications, transformations, and compositions, focusing on the desired output rather than the specific steps to achieve it.

   Example (in Haskell):

```
-- Declarative Haskell function to calculate the factorial of a non-negative integer
factorial :: Integer -> Integer
factorial n = product [1..n]
```

4. **Logic Programming Languages:**

   Logic programming languages, such as Prolog, embody the declarative programming paradigm by allowing developers to specify logical rules and relationships between entities. Programs written in logic programming languages describe the problem domain using rules and constraints, and the interpreter or compiler determines how to derive solutions based on the specified logic.

   Example (in Prolog):

```
% Declarative Prolog predicate to define the relationship between siblings
sibling(X, Y) :-
parent(Z, X),
parent(Z, Y),
X \= Y.
```

5. HTML (HyperText Markup Language) and CSS (Cascading Style Sheets):

HTML and CSS are declarative languages used for describing the structure and presentation of web pages, respectively. HTML specifies the semantic structure of web content, while CSS defines the visual appearance and layout. Developers describe the desired structure and styling of web elements using HTML and CSS, and web browsers interpret these declarations to render the page accordingly.

Example (in HTML and CSS):

```html
<!-- Declarative HTML markup for a simple web page -->
<!DOCTYPE html>
<html>
<head>
<title>Declarative Example</title>
<link rel="stylesheet" type="text/css" href="styles.css">
</head>
<body>
<h1>Welcome to Declarative Programming</h1>
<p>This is an example of declarative programming.</p>
</body>
</html>
/* Declarative CSS styles for the HTML markup */
body {
font-family: Arial, sans-serif;
background-color: #f0f0f0;
}
h1 {
color: #333;
}
p {
color: #666;
}
```

Declarative programming is a powerful paradigm for expressing computation in a concise, expressive, and maintainable manner. By focusing on what needs to be accomplished rather than how to accomplish it, declarative programming enables developers to describe complex systems and processes using high-level abstractions and domain-specific languages. Whether through SQL for database queries, functional programming for algorithmic computations, logic programming for rule-based systems, or HTML/CSS for web development, declarative programming provides a versatile approach to problem-solving in various domains.

5. Procedural Programming Paradigm:

Procedural programming is a programming paradigm that focuses on breaking down a program into smaller, reusable procedures or subroutines. These procedures encapsulate a series of instructions to perform a specific task, promoting code reusability, modularity, and maintainability. Procedural programming emphasizes sequential execution, control flow structures, and variable manipulation. Here, we explore the key aspects of the procedural programming paradigm with examples to illustrate its characteristics and applications.

1. **Procedures and Functions:**

   In procedural programming, procedures (also known as functions or subroutines) are the building blocks of a program. A procedure is a self-contained block of code that performs a specific task or computation. Procedures can accept parameters as inputs and return values as outputs, allowing for modular and reusable code.

   Example (in C):

```c
// Procedural function to calculate the factorial of a non-negative integer
int factorial(int n) {
int result = 1;
for (int i = 1; i <= n; i++) {
```

```
result *= i;
}
return result;
}
```

2. **Sequential Execution:**

   Procedural programming follows a sequential execution model, where statements are executed in the order they appear in the program. Control flows from one statement to the next, with the program executing each instruction sequentially until reaching the end or encountering a branching or looping construct.

   Example (in Python):

```python
# Procedural code to print a list of numbers
def print_numbers():
for i in range(1, 6):
print(i)
# Call the function to print numbers
print_numbers()
```

3. **Control Flow Structures:** Procedural programming employs control flow structures such as conditionals (if-else statements), loops (for, while), and branching (goto statements) to control the flow of execution within a program. These structures determine the order in which statements are executed based on specific conditions or iterations.

   Example (in C):

```c
// Procedural code to determine if a number is even or odd
#include <stdio.h>
void check_even_odd(int num) {
if (num % 2 == 0) {
printf("%d is even\n", num);
} else {
printf("%d is odd\n", num);
}
}
int main() {
```

```
int number = 7;
check_even_odd(number);
return 0;
}
```

4. **Data Abstraction:**

Procedural programming emphasizes data abstraction through the use of variables to store and manipulate data. Variables represent values that can be modified during program execution, allowing for the storage of intermediate results and input/output operations.

Example (in Pascal):

```pascal
// Procedural code to calculate the area of a rectangle
program CalculateArea;
var
length, width, area: integer;
begin
length := 5;
width := 4;
area := length * width;
writeln('Area: ', area);
end.
```

5. **Example Application - Algorithmic Problem Solving:**

Procedural programming is well-suited for algorithmic problem-solving tasks, such as mathematical computations, sorting algorithms, and data processing. Its emphasis on sequential execution, control flow structures, and modularity makes it suitable for writing efficient and maintainable code to solve a wide range of problems.

The procedural programming paradigm provides a structured and modular approach to building software systems by emphasizing procedures, sequential execution, control flow structures, and data abstraction. By breaking down programs into smaller, reusable procedures, procedural programming facilitates code reusability, modularity, and maintainability. Whether through algorithmic problem solving, system scripting, or application development, procedural programming offers a versatile approach to software development across various domains and applications.

Conclusion:

Understanding different programming paradigms provides programmers with a diverse set of tools and techniques for solving problems effectively. By exploring imperative, functional, object-oriented, declarative, and procedural programming paradigms, programmers can select the most suitable approach for designing scalable, maintainable, and efficient software solutions across various domains and applications.

Introduction to Python Programming:

Python is a versatile, high-level programming language known for its simplicity, readability, and flexibility. It has gained immense popularity in various domains, including web development, data science, artificial intelligence, and automation.

1. **Python's Key Features:**

Simple and Readable Syntax:

Python's syntax is designed to be intuitive and easy to read, making it accessible for beginners and experienced programmers alike.

Python's simple and readable syntax is one of its most celebrated features. It contributes significantly to Python's popularity among beginners and seasoned developers alike.

1. **Indentation-based Structure:**

Python's use of indentation for code structure eliminates the need for explicit block delimiters like curly braces {} or **begin** and **end** keywords. This results in cleaner and more visually appealing code, enhancing readability.

Example:

```
# Python code with indentation-based structure
for i in range(5):
if i % 2 == 0:
print(i, "is even")
else:
print(i, "is odd")
```

2. **Minimalistic Syntax:**

Python employs a minimalist syntax that emphasizes clarity and conciseness. This means that developers can achieve complex tasks with fewer lines of code compared to other languages, reducing cognitive load and making code easier to understand.

Example:

```
# Python code demonstrating minimalistic syntax
numbers = [1, 2, 3, 4, 5]
squared_numbers = [x ** 2 for x in numbers if x % 2 == 0]
print(squared_numbers)
```

3. **Readability through English-like Constructs:**

Python's syntax is designed to resemble natural language constructs, making it intuitive and easy to understand for both programmers and non-programmers. This readability feature reduces the learning curve for beginners and promotes collaboration among team members.

Example:

```
# Python code with English-like constructs
def calculate_area(length, width):
    """

    Function to calculate the area of a rectangle.
    """

    return length * width
```

4. **Explicitness and Clarity:**

Python prioritizes explicitness and clarity, discouraging cryptic or ambiguous syntax. This ensures that code is self-explanatory and understandable even to someone unfamiliar with the project, enhancing maintainability and code quality.

Example:

# Python code demonstrating explicitness and clarity
if condition:
perform_action()
else:
handle_alternative()

5. **Built-in Documentation Support:**

Python encourages documentation as part of its syntax. Docstrings, which are string literals used to document modules, classes, functions, and methods, facilitate automatic generation of documentation and provide valuable insights into the purpose and usage of code elements.

Example:

# Python code with built-in documentation support
def calculate_area(length, width):
"""

Function to calculate the area of a rectangle.
Parameters:
length (float): The length of the rectangle.
width (float): The width of the rectangle.
Returns:
float: The area of the rectangle.
"""

return length * width

Python's simple and readable syntax is a defining characteristic of the language. By leveraging indentation-based structure, minimalist syntax, English-like constructs, explicitness, clarity, and built-in documentation support, Python ensures that code is easy to write, understand, and maintain. These features contribute to Python's widespread adoption across various domains and its appeal to developers of all skill levels.

High-Level Language:

Python abstracts low-level details, allowing developers to focus on solving problems rather than managing memory or hardware resources.

Python is renowned for being a high-level programming language, which means it abstracts away low-level details such as memory management and hardware interaction, allowing developers to focus on solving problems at a higher level of abstraction

1. **Abstraction of Low-Level Details:**

   Python shields developers from the complexities of low-level tasks such as memory management, pointer arithmetic, and hardware-specific optimizations. This abstraction enables programmers to write code that is more concise, readable, and platform-independent.

   Example:

   ```python
   # Python code to calculate the sum of elements in a list
   numbers = [1, 2, 3, 4, 5]
   total = sum(numbers)
   print("Sum of numbers:", total)
   ```

2. **Dynamic Typing and Automatic Memory Management:**

   Python is dynamically typed, meaning that variables do not need to be declared with a specific type before use. The interpreter determines the type of a variable at runtime, providing flexibility and reducing the cognitive overhead of type declarations. Additionally, Python features automatic memory management through garbage collection, freeing developers from manual memory allocation and deallocation.

   Example:

   ```python
   # Python code demonstrating dynamic typing
   x = 10 # x is an integer
   ```

```
x = "Hello" # Now x is a string
x = [1, 2, 3] # Now x is a list
```

3. **Extensive Standard Library:**

Python comes with a comprehensive standard library that provides modules and packages for a wide range of tasks, including file I/O, networking, data manipulation, and more. This rich collection of tools enables developers to build complex applications without relying heavily on external libraries.

Example:

```
# Python code using the datetime module from the standard library
import datetime
# Get the current date and time
current_time = datetime.datetime.now()
print("Current time:", current_time)
```

4. **Interpreted and Interactive Execution:**

Python is an interpreted language, meaning that code is executed line by line by the Python interpreter. This allows for rapid development and testing, as changes to code can be immediately executed and results observed. Python also supports interactive mode, where commands can be entered directly into the interpreter for immediate execution and feedback.

Example:

```
# Python code demonstrating interactive execution
>>> x = 5
>>> y = 10
>>> x + y
15
```

5. **Platform Independence:**

Python code is highly portable and can run on various operating systems, including Windows, macOS, and Linux, without modification. This platform independence makes Python an ideal choice for developing cross-platform applications and ensures compatibility across different environments.

Example:

# Python code demonstrating platform independence
import os
print("Operating system:", os.name)

Python's status as a high-level programming language offers numerous benefits to developers, including abstraction of low-level details, dynamic typing, automatic memory management, an extensive standard library, interpreted and interactive execution, and platform independence. These features contribute to Python's popularity and versatility, making it suitable for a wide range of applications, from web development and data science to automation and artificial intelligence. Python's high-level nature allows developers to focus on solving problems efficiently and effectively, without being bogged down by implementation details.

Interpreted and Interactive:

Python is an interpreted language, meaning that code is executed line by line by an interpreter. It also supports interactive mode, allowing users to execute code interactively and see immediate results.

Python is an interpreted and interactive programming language, which means that code is executed line by line by an interpreter, and developers can interactively execute code and receive immediate feedback.

Interpreted Execution:

Python is an interpreted language, meaning that Python code is executed directly by an interpreter, rather than being compiled into machine code beforehand. The Python interpreter reads and executes Python code line by line, translating each statement into machine instructions on-the-fly.

Python's interpreted execution is a fundamental aspect of the language that contributes to its flexibility, ease of use, and popularity

1. **Interpreted Execution Defined:**

   Interpreted execution refers to the process of translating and executing code statements directly by an interpreter at runtime, without the need for prior compilation into machine code. In Python, the Python interpreter reads Python code line by line and executes each statement sequentially.

2. **Flexibility and Rapid Development:**

   Because Python code is executed by an interpreter rather than being compiled, developers can write and execute Python code quickly and easily. This flexibility enables rapid development and iteration, as changes to the code can be immediately tested and observed without the overhead of compilation steps.

   Example:

```python
# Python code demonstrating rapid development with interpreted execution
def greet(name):
return "Hello, " + name
# Call the function and print the result
print(greet("Alice"))
```

3. **Interactive Mode:**

   Python's interactive mode allows developers to enter Python commands directly into the interpreter and see the results immediately. This interactive environment is invaluable for testing code snippets, exploring language features, and debugging, as developers can experiment with Python syntax and expressions in real-time.

   Example:

```
$ python
Python 3.9.7 (default, Sep 3 2021, 09:25:36)
[GCC 10.3.0] on linux
Type "help", "copyright", "credits" or "license" for more information.
>>> x = 5
```

```
>>> y = 10
>>> x + y
15
```

4. **Platform Independence:**

Python's interpreted execution makes it highly portable across different operating systems and platforms. Because Python code is executed by the interpreter, rather than directly interacting with hardware, Python programs can run on any platform that has a compatible Python interpreter installed.

Example:

```
# Python code demonstrating platform independence with inter-
preted execution
import os
print("Operating system:", os.name)
```

5. **Easy Deployment:**

Deploying Python applications is straightforward due to the interpreted nature of the language. Unlike compiled languages, Python code does not need to be compiled into machine code before deployment. Instead, developers can distribute Python scripts or packages directly, and users can execute them using the Python interpreter on their system.

Example:

```
# Python script to calculate the factorial of a number
def factorial(n):
if n == 0:
return 1
else:
return n * factorial(n-1)
# Call the function and print the result
print("Factorial of 5:", factorial(5))
```

Python's interpreted execution is a key feature that underpins its flexibility, ease of use, and versatility. The ability to write, test, and execute Python code quickly and easily with an interpreter enables rapid development, interactive exploration, platform independence, and easy deployment of Python applications. Interpreted execution is a cornerstone of Python's success as a programming language and plays a vital role in its widespread adoption across various domains and industries.

Dynamic Typing:

Python is dynamically typed, meaning that variable types are determined at runtime. Developers do not need to declare variable types explicitly, enhancing flexibility and productivity.

Dynamic typing is a fundamental feature of Python that allows variables to change types dynamically during runtime.

1. **Dynamic Typing Defined:**

   In Python, variables are not bound to a specific data type at compile-time; instead, their type is determined at runtime based on the value assigned to them. This means that a variable can hold values of different types at different points in the program's execution.

2. **Flexibility and Expressiveness:**

   Dynamic typing in Python provides developers with flexibility and expressiveness when writing code. Variables can be assigned values of any type without the need for explicit type declarations, making Python code concise and readable.

   Example:

   ```python
   # Python code demonstrating dynamic typing
   x = 5 # x is an integer
   x = "Hello" # Now x is a string
   x = [1, 2, 3] # Now x is a list
   ```

3. **Reduced Boilerplate:**

   Dynamic typing reduces the amount of boilerplate code required in Python programs compared to statically-typed languages. Because variables do not need to be declared with specific types, developers can focus on solving problems rather than managing type declarations.

Example:

```python
# Python code demonstrating reduced boilerplate with dynamic typing
def add_numbers(a, b):
return a + b
result = add_numbers(5, 10) # Both parameters are integers
print("Result:", result)
result = add_numbers("Hello", "World") # Both parameters are strings
print("Result:", result)
```

4. **Improved Productivity:**

Dynamic typing enhances developer productivity by allowing for faster prototyping and iteration. Developers can write and test code more quickly since they don't need to worry about type declarations or conversions.

Example:

```python
# Python code demonstrating improved productivity with dynamic typing
def calculate_area(length, width):
return length * width
# No need to specify types for length and width
area = calculate_area(5, 10)
print("Area:", area)
```

5. **Increased Readability:**

Dynamic typing contributes to the readability of Python code by reducing clutter and unnecessary type information. Python code is often more concise and understandable since variable names convey their purpose without additional type annotations.

Example:

```python
# Python code demonstrating increased readability with dynamic typing
def concatenate_strings(a, b):
```

```
return a + b
# No need to specify types for a and b
result = concatenate_strings("Hello", "World")
print("Result:", result)
```

Dynamic typing is a core feature of Python that provides flexibility, expressiveness, reduced boilerplate, improved productivity, and increased readability. By allowing variables to change types dynamically during runtime and eliminating the need for explicit type declarations, dynamic typing enables developers to write concise, readable, and maintainable code. Dynamic typing is a key factor in Python's popularity and widespread adoption across various domains and industries.

Rich Standard Library:

Python comes with a comprehensive standard library, providing modules and packages for various tasks such as file I/O, networking, and data manipulation.

Python's rich standard library is one of its most powerful features, providing a vast collection of modules and packages that extend the language's capabilities for various tasks.

1. **Abundance of Modules and Packages:**

    Python's standard library encompasses a wide range of modules and packages that cater to diverse programming needs. These modules cover areas such as file I/O, networking, data manipulation, mathematics, and much more, eliminating the need for developers to reinvent the wheel for common tasks.

    Example:

    ```
    # Python code utilizing the os module for interacting with the
    operating system
    import os
    # Get the current working directory
    current_dir = os.getcwd()
    print("Current directory:", current_dir)
    # List files in the current directory
    ```

```
files = os.listdir()
print("Files in current directory:", files)
```

2. **Built-in Data Structures and Algorithms:**

Python's standard library includes built-in data structures and algorithms that facilitate efficient and scalable solutions to common problems. These data structures, such as lists, dictionaries, sets, and tuples, provide essential building blocks for developing robust applications.

Example:

```
# Python code demonstrating the use of built-in data structures
# Create a list of numbers
numbers = [1, 2, 3, 4, 5]
# Use a dictionary to store key-value pairs
student = {'name': 'Alice', 'age': 25, 'grade': 'A'}
# Create a set of unique elements
unique_numbers = {1, 2, 3, 4, 5}
# Use tuples to represent immutable sequences
point = (10, 20)
```

3. **Support for File I/O Operations:**

Python's standard library offers robust support for file input and output operations, allowing developers to read from and write to files seamlessly. Modules such as **open**, **os**, and **shutil** provide functionalities for file handling, directory manipulation, and file system operations.

Example:

```
# Python code demonstrating file I/O operations
# Read content from a file
with open('example.txt', 'r') as file:
content = file.read()
print("File content:", content)
# Write content to a new file
with open('new_file.txt', 'w') as file:
file.write("Hello, World!")
```

4. **Networking and Internet Protocols:**

Python's standard library includes modules for networking and internet protocols, enabling developers to create networked applications, interact with web services, and implement client-server architectures. Modules such as **socket**, **http**, and **urllib** facilitate network communication and web scraping tasks.

Example:

```python
# Python code demonstrating networking with the socket module
import socket
# Create a socket object
server_socket = socket.socket(socket.AF_INET, socket.SOCK_STREAM)
# Bind the socket to a specific address and port
server_socket.bind(('localhost', 12345))
# Listen for incoming connections
server_socket.listen(5)
print("Server is listening for connections...")
# Accept incoming connections
client_socket, address = server_socket.accept()
print("Connection established with:", address)
# Close the connection
client_socket.close()
server_socket.close()
```

5. **Extensive Support for Data Manipulation and Analysis:**

Python's standard library offers modules for data manipulation and analysis, making it well-suited for tasks such as data cleaning, transformation, and visualization. Modules such as **csv**, **json**, **datetime**, and **math** provide functionalities for working with different data formats and performing mathematical computations.

Example:

```python
# Python code demonstrating data manipulation with the csv module
```

```
import csv
# Read data from a CSV file
with open('data.csv', 'r') as file:
reader = csv.reader(file)
for row in reader:
print(row)
# Write data to a new CSV file
data = [['Name', 'Age'], ['Alice', 25], ['Bob', 30], ['Charlie', 35]]
with open('new_data.csv', 'w', newline='') as file:
writer = csv.writer(file)
writer.writerows(data)
```

Python's rich standard library is a cornerstone of the language's success, providing developers with a vast array of modules and packages to tackle a wide range of programming tasks. From file I/O operations and networking to data manipulation and analysis, Python's standard library offers comprehensive support for various programming needs, eliminating the need for external dependencies and accelerating the development process. The richness of Python's standard library contributes to its versatility, ease of use, and widespread adoption across different domains

2. Python Syntax:

Indentation:

Python uses indentation to define blocks of code, such as loops, conditionals, and functions. Consistent indentation is crucial for code readability and structure.

Python's indentation-based syntax is a distinctive feature that sets it apart from other programming languages. In Python, indentation is not merely a stylistic choice but a fundamental aspect of the language's syntax, used to denote block structures such as loops, conditionals, and function definitions.

1. Indentation as Block Structure:

In Python, indentation is used to indicate the beginning and end of blocks of code. Unlike languages that use braces {} or keywords like **begin** and **end** to denote blocks, Python relies on consistent indentation to define the scope of statements within a block. This results in cleaner, more readable code and helps maintain a consistent coding style across projects.

Example:

```python
# Python code demonstrating indentation for block structure
if condition:
# Indented block
print("Condition is true")
else:
# Indented block
print("Condition is false")
```

2. **Consistency in Indentation:**

Consistent indentation is crucial in Python to ensure code clarity and maintainability. All statements within the same block must be indented by the same amount, typically using four spaces per level of indentation. Mixing tabs and spaces for indentation or using inconsistent indentation levels can lead to syntax errors or unexpected behavior.

Example:

```python
# Python code demonstrating consistent indentation
if condition:
# Indented block
print("Condition is true")
print("Inside the if block")
else:
# Inconsistent indentation - may cause syntax error
print("Condition is false")
```

3. **Nested Block Structures:**

Python's indentation syntax supports nested block structures, allowing for the nesting of loops, conditionals, and function definitions within one another. This hierarchical organization of code enhances readability and makes it easier to understand the relationships between different parts of the program.

Example:

```python
# Python code demonstrating nested block structures
for i in range(3):
# Outer loop
for j in range(3):
# Inner loop
print(i, j)
```

4. **No Explicit Block Delimiters:**

Unlike languages such as C, Java, or JavaScript, Python does not use explicit block delimiters like braces {} to denote blocks of code. Instead, indentation serves as the sole indicator of block structure. This leads to cleaner, more concise code and reduces the potential for errors caused by mismatched braces.

Example:

```python
# Python code demonstrating absence of explicit block delimiters
if condition:
print("Block 1")
else:
print("Block 2")
```

5. **Readability and Maintainability:**

Python's indentation-based syntax enhances code readability and maintainability by enforcing a consistent and visually appealing coding style. Proper indentation helps developers quickly understand the structure of the code and identify logical blocks, reducing the cognitive load required to comprehend the program's logic.

Example:

```python
# Python code demonstrating readability and maintainability
def calculate_total(items):
total = 0
for item in items:
```

```
# Indented block
total += item
return total
```

Python's indentation-based syntax is a defining feature of the language, emphasizing readability, maintainability, and code consistency. By using indentation to denote block structure, Python promotes clean, visually appealing code and discourages cluttered or convoluted syntax. Proper indentation is crucial in Python to ensure code clarity and avoid syntax errors, making it an essential aspect of mastering the language.

Variables and Data Types:

Variables in Python are dynamically typed and do not require explicit declaration. Python supports various data types, including integers, floats, strings, lists, tuples, dictionaries, and sets.

In Python, variables and data types are fundamental components of the language syntax. Understanding how to declare variables, assign values, and work with different data types is essential for effective Python programming.

1. **Variables and Assignment:**

   In Python, variables are used to store data values. Unlike some statically-typed languages, Python does not require explicit variable declaration with a specific data type. Variables are created when they are first assigned a value, and their type is dynamically determined based on the assigned value.

   Example:

   ```
   # Python code demonstrating variable assignment
   x = 5 # Integer variable
   name = "Alice" # String variable
   is_active = True # Boolean variable
   ```

2. **Data Types:**

   Python supports various built-in data types, including integers, floating-point numbers, strings, booleans, lists, tuples, dictionaries, and more. Each data type has its characteristics and is suited for specific tasks, allowing for versatile and expressive programming.

Example:

```python
# Python code demonstrating different data types
integer_var = 10 # Integer
float_var = 3.14 # Float
string_var = "Hello, World!" # String
boolean_var = True # Boolean
list_var = [1, 2, 3, 4, 5] # List
tuple_var = (1, 2, 3) # Tuple
dictionary_var = {'name': 'Alice', 'age': 30} # Dictionary
```

3. **Type Conversion:**

Python allows for implicit and explicit type conversion between different data types. Implicit conversion, also known as type coercion, occurs automatically when performing operations involving different types. Explicit conversion, on the other hand, involves using built-in functions like **int()**, **float()**, **str()**, etc., to convert between data types explicitly.

Example:

```python
# Python code demonstrating type conversion
x = 10
y = 3.5
# Implicit conversion
result = x + y # Integer is implicitly converted to float
print("Result:", result)
# Explicit conversion
x_str = str(x) # Convert integer to string
y_int = int(y) # Convert float to integer
```

4. **Variable Naming Convention:**

Python follows specific conventions for naming variables to improve code readability and maintainability. Variable names should be descriptive, meaningful, and follow a consistent naming convention, such as lowercase with underscores (**snake_case**) for regular variables and uppercase for constants.

Example:

```
# Python code demonstrating variable naming convention
first_name = "Alice"
last_name = "Smith"
age = 30
PI = 3.14
```

5. **Mutable vs. Immutable Data Types:**

In Python, some data types are mutable, meaning their values can be changed after creation, while others are immutable, meaning their values cannot be changed. Understanding the mutability of data types is essential for writing efficient and bug-free code.

Example:

```
# Python code demonstrating mutable and immutable data types
# Immutable data types: int, float, string, tuple
x = 10
y = (1, 2, 3)
# Mutable data types: list, dictionary
numbers = [1, 2, 3, 4, 5]
person = {'name': 'Alice', 'age': 30}
```

Python syntax for variables and data types is straightforward yet powerful, offering flexibility and expressiveness for programming tasks. By understanding how to declare variables, work with different data types, perform type conversion, and follow naming conventions, Python developers can write clear, efficient, and maintainable code. Mastery of Python's variables and data types is foundational to becoming proficient in the language and unlocking its full potential for various applications.

Control Flow Structures:

Python supports control flow structures such as if-else statements, for and while loops, and try-except blocks for exception handling.

Control flow structures in Python are essential for defining the flow of execution in a program. They allow developers to execute certain code blocks conditionally, repeatedly, or selectively based on different criteria.

1. **Conditional Statements (if-elif-else):**

   Conditional statements in Python allow for executing different blocks of code based on specified conditions. The **if**, **elif** (else if), and **else** keywords are used to define conditional blocks. Python's indentation-based syntax is crucial for delimiting these blocks.

   Example:

```python
# Python code demonstrating conditional statements
x = 10
if x > 0:
print("x is positive")
elif x < 0:
print("x is negative")
else:
print("x is zero")
```

2. **Loops (for and while):**

   Python supports two main types of loops: **for** loops and **while** loops. **for** loops iterate over a sequence of elements, such as lists or tuples, while **while** loops execute a block of code repeatedly as long as a specified condition is true.

   Example:

```python
# Python code demonstrating for loop
numbers = [1, 2, 3, 4, 5]
for num in numbers:
print(num)
# Python code demonstrating while loop
x = 0
while x < 5:
```

```
print(x)
x += 1
```

3. **Loop Control Statements (break, continue, and pass):**

Python provides loop control statements to modify the behavior of loops. **break** terminates the loop prematurely, **continue** skips the current iteration and moves to the next one, and **pass** is a placeholder that does nothing.

Example:

```
# Python code demonstrating loop control statements
numbers = [1, 2, 3, 4, 5]
for num in numbers:
if num == 3:
break # Terminate the loop when num is 3
print(num)
# Python code demonstrating continue statement
for num in numbers:
if num % 2 == 0:
continue # Skip even numbers
print(num)
```

4. **Iterating Over Sequences (range and enumerate):**

The **range()** function generates a sequence of numbers that can be used to iterate over a specific range. The **enumerate()** function is used to iterate over sequences while also keeping track of the index.

Example:

```
# Python code demonstrating range function
for i in range(5):
print(i)
# Python code demonstrating enumerate function
fruits = ['apple', 'banana', 'cherry']
for index, fruit in enumerate(fruits):
print(index, fruit)
```

5. **Ternary Operator (Conditional Expression):**

Python supports a concise syntax for conditional expressions, known as the ternary operator. It allows for writing conditional statements in a single line, which can be useful for assigning values based on conditions.

Example:

```
# Python code demonstrating ternary operator
x = 10
result = "Even" if x % 2 == 0 else "Odd"
print(result)
```

Control flow structures in Python, including conditional statements, loops, loop control statements, and iterator functions, are essential for controlling the flow of execution in Python programs. By understanding and mastering these constructs, developers can create powerful and efficient programs that perform various tasks, from simple condition checking to complex iteration and manipulation of data structures. Python's clear and concise syntax for control flow structures contributes to its readability, maintainability, and versatility as a programming language.

Functions:

Functions in Python are defined using the **def** keyword and can accept parameters and return values. Python also supports lambda functions for anonymous functions.

Functions are a fundamental concept in Python programming, allowing developers to encapsulate reusable blocks of code and organize their programs effectively.

1. **Function Declaration and Definition:**

   In Python, functions are declared using the **def** keyword, followed by the function name and a pair of parentheses containing optional parameters. The function body is indented below the declaration, and the **return** statement is used to specify the value returned by the function.

   Example:

```python
# Python code demonstrating function declaration and definition
def greet(name):
return "Hello, " + name
# Call the function and print the result
message = greet("Alice")
print(message)
```

2. **Function Parameters and Arguments:**

Python functions can accept parameters, which are placeholders for values passed to the function when it is called. Parameters can have default values, making them optional. Arguments are the actual values supplied to the function when it is called.

Example:

```python
# Python code demonstrating function parameters and arguments
def add_numbers(a, b=0):
return a + b
# Call the function with different arguments
result1 = add_numbers(5, 3)
result2 = add_numbers(10)
print("Result 1:", result1)
print("Result 2:", result2)
```

3. **Keyword Arguments:**

Python allows passing arguments to functions using keyword arguments, where the argument is explicitly specified by its parameter name. This allows for more readable function calls and enables passing arguments in any order.

Example:

```python
# Python code demonstrating keyword arguments
def greet(name, greeting="Hello"):
return greeting + ", " + name
# Call the function with keyword arguments
message1 = greet(name="Alice", greeting="Hi")
message2 = greet(greeting="Good morning", name="Bob")
```

```
print("Message 1:", message1)
print("Message 2:", message2)
```

4. **Variable-Length Arguments:**

Python functions can accept a variable number of arguments using the ***args** and ****kwargs** syntax. ***args** collects additional positional arguments into a tuple, while ****kwargs** collects additional keyword arguments into a dictionary.

Example:

```
# Python code demonstrating variable-length arguments
def calculate_sum(*args):
return sum(args)
result = calculate_sum(1, 2, 3, 4, 5)
print("Sum:", result)
```

5. **Anonymous Functions (Lambda Functions):**

Python supports the creation of anonymous functions using the **lambda** keyword. Lambda functions are small, inline functions that can take any number of arguments but can only contain a single expression.

Example:

```
# Python code demonstrating lambda functions
square = lambda x: x ** 2
result = square(5)
print("Square of 5:", result)
```

6. **Scope of Variables:**

Python follows a scope-based variable resolution mechanism, where variables defined inside a function are local to that function by default. However, variables declared in the outer scope can be accessed within the function using the **global** keyword.

Example:

```
# Python code demonstrating variable scope
x = 10 # Global variable
def print_x():
```

```
print("Value of x:", x) # Accessing global variable
print_x()
```

Functions are essential building blocks in Python programming, enabling code reuse, modularity, and organization. By understanding how to declare and define functions, work with function parameters and arguments, and utilize advanced features such as keyword arguments, variable-length arguments, and lambda functions, Python developers can write clear, concise, and efficient code. Functions play a crucial role in Python programming, promoting good coding practices, readability, and maintainability of codebases.

Modules and Packages:

Python allows developers to organize code into modules and packages, facilitating code reuse and modularity. Modules are Python files containing functions, classes, or variables, while packages are directories containing multiple modules.

In Python, modules and packages are key components for organizing and structuring code into reusable and maintainable units. They facilitate code modularity, encapsulation, and reuse, making it easier to manage large-scale projects.

1. **Modules:**

   Modules in Python are files containing Python code that define functions, classes, and variables. They allow for code organization and reuse by providing a way to split code into separate files. Modules are imported into other Python scripts to access their functionality.

   Example: Consider a module named "**math_operations.py**" containing mathematical functions:

```
# math_operations.py
def add(a, b):
return a + b
def subtract(a, b):
return a – b
```

You can import and use this module in another script as follows:

```
# main.py
import math_operations
result = math_operations.add(5, 3)
print("Addition:", result)
result = math_operations.subtract(10, 7)
print("Subtraction:", result)
```

2. **Packages:**

Packages in Python are directories that contain multiple modules and an additional '**__init__.py**' file. The' **__init__.py**' file can be empty or contain initialization code for the package. Packages help organize modules hierarchically, providing a namespace for related functionality.

Example: Consider a package named '**geometry**' containing modules for geometric calculations:

```
geometry/
__init__.py
shapes.py
calculations.py
```

You can import and use modules from this package as follows:

```
# Using modules from the geometry package
from geometry import shapes, calculations
area = shapes.rectangle_area(5, 3)
print("Rectangle Area:", area)
volume = calculations.cube_volume(4)
print("Cube Volume:", volume)
```

3. **Importing Modules and Packages:**

Python provides various ways to import modules and packages, allowing for flexible usage depending on the requirements. You can import specific functions, import modules with an alias, import all contents of a module, or import modules from packages.

Example

```
# Importing specific functions from a module
```

```
from math_operations import add, subtract
result = add(5, 3)
# Importing a module with an alias
import math_operations as mo
result = mo.subtract(10, 7)
# Importing all contents of a module
from math_operations import *
result = subtract(10, 7)
# Importing modules from a package
from geometry import shapes
```

4. **Built-in Modules:**

Python comes with a rich standard library containing built-in modules for various tasks, such as file I/O, string manipulation, networking, and more. These modules provide essential functionalities without the need for external dependencies.

Example:

```
# Using built-in modules
import os
current_dir = os.getcwd()
print("Current Directory:", current_dir)
import random
random_number = random.randint(1, 100)
print("Random Number:", random_number)
```

5. **Creating and Distributing Packages:**

Python provides tools like **setuptools** and **pip** for creating and distributing packages. By following packaging conventions and using these tools, developers can package their code for distribution and installation by others, facilitating code sharing and collaboration.

Modules and packages are indispensable tools in Python programming for organizing, structuring, and managing code effectively. By leveraging modules and packages, developers can create modular, reusable, and maintainable codebases, enabling code reuse, collaboration, and scalability. Understanding how to import modules, work with packages, and utilize built-in modules empowers Python developers to build robust and efficient applications for a wide range of domains and industries.

3. Python Applications:

Web Development:

Python is widely used for web development, with frameworks like Django and Flask offering powerful tools for building web applications, APIs, and backend services.

Python is a versatile programming language that is widely used in web development due to its simplicity, readability, and vast ecosystem of libraries and frameworks.

1. **Web Frameworks:**

   Python offers several web frameworks that simplify the process of building web applications by providing tools and libraries for handling HTTP requests, routing, database integration, templating, and more. Some popular Python web frameworks include Django, Flask, Pyramid, and FastAPI.

   Example:

   ```python
   # Example of a simple Flask web application
   from flask import Flask
   app = Flask(__name__)
   @app.route('/')
   def hello_world():
   return 'Hello, World!'
   if __name__ == '__main__':
   app.run()
   ```

2. **Django:**

   Django is a high-level Python web framework that encourages rapid development and clean, pragmatic design. It includes built-in features for authentication, URL routing, database management, and templating, making it ideal for building complex web applications.

Example:

```python
# Example of a simple Django web application
from django.http import HttpResponse
from django.urls import path
from django.conf import settings
from django.conf.urls.static import static
from django.shortcuts import render
def index(request):
return HttpResponse("Hello, World!")
urlpatterns = [
path(", index),
]
if __name__ == "__main__":
from django.core.management import execute_from_command_line
execute_from_command_line(sys.argv)
```

3. **Flask:**

Flask is a lightweight web framework for Python that emphasizes simplicity and flexibility. It provides a minimalistic approach to web development, allowing developers to build web applications quickly and easily with a small footprint.

Example:

```python
# Example of a simple Flask web application
from flask import Flask
app = Flask(__name__)
@app.route('/')
def hello_world():
return 'Hello, World!'
if __name__ == '__main__':
app.run()
```

4. **FastAPI:**

FastAPI is a modern web framework for building APIs with

Python, known for its high performance and automatic genera-tion of OpenAPI documentation. It leverages Python type anno-tations for input validation and automatic serialization, resulting in fast and efficient API development.

Example:

```python
# Example of a simple FastAPI application
from fastapi import FastAPI
app = FastAPI()
@app.get("/")
async def read_root():
return {"message": "Hello, World"}
```

5. **Web Scraping:**

Python's rich ecosystem of libraries makes it an excellent choice for web scraping, which involves extracting data from websites. Libraries like BeautifulSoup and Scrapy provide powerful tools for parsing HTML and XML documents, making it easy to retrieve and process data from the web.

Example:

```python
# Example of web scraping using BeautifulSoup
import requests
from bs4 import BeautifulSoup
url = 'https://www.example.com'
response = requests.get(url)
soup = BeautifulSoup(response.text, 'html.parser')
# Extracting all the links from the webpage
links = soup.find_all('a')
for link in links:
print(link.get('href'))
```

6. **Deployment:**

Python web applications can be deployed on various platforms, in-cluding traditional web servers like Apache and Nginx, cloud platforms like AWS and Google Cloud Platform, and container orchestration platforms like Docker and Kubernetes. Tools like Flask, Django, and FastAPI provide built-in support for deployment and scaling.

Python's versatility, simplicity, and extensive ecosystem make it an ideal choice for web development. Whether building simple websites, complex web applications, or APIs, Python offers powerful frameworks, libraries, and tools that streamline the development process and enable developers to create robust and scalable web solutions. With its wide adoption in the industry and strong community support, Python continues to be a top choice for web developers worldwide.

Data Science and Machine Learning:

Python has become the de facto language for data science and machine learning due to libraries such as NumPy, Pandas, Matplotlib, and scikit-learn, which provide robust tools for data manipulation, analysis, visualization, and machine learning modeling.

Python has become the lingua franca of data science and machine learning due to its simplicity, versatility, and extensive ecosystem of libraries and tools.

1. **Data Analysis and Visualization:**

   Python offers powerful libraries like NumPy, pandas, and Matplotlib for data analysis and visualization. NumPy provides support for multi-dimensional arrays and mathematical operations, pandas offers data structures and tools for data manipulation and analysis, while Matplotlib enables the creation of various types of plots and visualizations.

   Example:

   ```
   # Example of data analysis and visualization using pandas and Matplotlib
   import pandas as pd
   import matplotlib.pyplot as plt
   # Load data into a pandas DataFrame
   data = pd.read_csv('data.csv')
   # Analyze and visualize data
   ```

```
data.describe()
data.plot(x='Date', y='Value')
plt.show()
```

2. **Machine Learning:**

Python's scikit-learn library provides a wide range of algorithms and tools for machine learning tasks such as classification, regression, clustering, and dimensionality reduction. Scikit-learn is built on top of NumPy, SciPy, and matplotlib, making it easy to integrate with other data science libraries.

Example:

```python
# Example of machine learning using scikit-learn
from sklearn.model_selection import train_test_split
from sklearn.linear_model import LogisticRegression
from sklearn.metrics import accuracy_score
# Load dataset
X, y = load_dataset('data.csv')
# Split data into training and testing sets
X_train, X_test, y_train, y_test = train_test_split(X, y, test_size=0.2)
# Initialize and train model
model = LogisticRegression()
model.fit(X_train, y_train)
# Make predictions
predictions = model.predict(X_test)
# Evaluate model accuracy
accuracy = accuracy_score(y_test, predictions)
print("Accuracy:", accuracy)
```

3. **Deep Learning:**

Python's TensorFlow and PyTorch libraries are widely used for deep learning tasks, such as building and training neural networks for image classification, natural language processing, and reinforcement learning. These libraries provide high-level APIs for building and training neural networks efficiently.

Example:

```python
# Example of deep learning using TensorFlow
import tensorflow as tf
# Define a simple neural network
model = tf.keras.Sequential([
tf.keras.layers.Dense(128, activation='relu', input_shape=(784,)),
tf.keras.layers.Dropout(0.2),
tf.keras.layers.Dense(10, activation='softmax')
])
# Compile the model
model.compile(optimizer='adam',
loss='sparse_categorical_crossentropy',
metrics=['accuracy'])
# Train the model
model.fit(X_train, y_train, epochs=5)
# Evaluate the model
loss, accuracy = model.evaluate(X_test, y_test)
print("Test Accuracy:", accuracy)
```

4. **Natural Language Processing (NLP):**

   Python's NLTK (Natural Language Toolkit) and spaCy libraries are widely used for natural language processing tasks such as tokenization, part-of-speech tagging, named entity recognition, sentiment analysis, and text classification.

   Example:

```python
# Example of natural language processing using spaCy
import spacy
# Load English language model
nlp = spacy.load('en_core_web_sm')
# Process text
doc = nlp("Apple is looking at buying U.K. startup for $1 billion")
for token in doc:
print(token.text, token.lemma_, token.pos_, token.tag_, to-
```

```
ken.dep_,
token.shape_, token.is_alpha, token.is_stop)
```

5. **Data Science Applications:**

Python is extensively used in various data science applications such as predictive modeling, recommendation systems, fraud detection, customer segmentation, and churn prediction. Its rich ecosystem of libraries and tools enables data scientists to tackle complex real-world problems efficiently.

Python's applications in data science and machine learning are vast and diverse, ranging from data analysis and visualization to machine learning, deep learning, natural language processing, and more. Its simplicity, versatility, and extensive library ecosystem make it the language of choice for data scientists and machine learning practitioners worldwide. By leveraging Python's rich ecosystem of libraries and tools, data scientists can tackle complex problems and extract valuable insights from data to drive decision-making and innovation across various domains and industries.

Artificial Intelligence and Natural Language Processing:

Python is extensively used in artificial intelligence and natural language processing applications, with libraries like TensorFlow, PyTorch, and NLTK enabling the development of advanced AI models and text processing algorithms.

Python is widely used in artificial intelligence (AI) and natural language processing (NLP) due to its simplicity, extensive libraries, and powerful frameworks.

1. **Natural Language Processing (NLP):**

   NLP involves the interaction between computers and human (natural) languages. Python offers several libraries and frameworks for NLP tasks such as tokenization, part-of-speech tagging, named entity recognition, sentiment analysis, and text classification.

Example:

```
# Example of NLP using NLTK for tokenization and part-of-speech tagging
import nltk
# Download NLTK resources
nltk.download('punkt')
nltk.download('averaged_perceptron_tagger')
# Tokenization
text = "Natural language processing (NLP) is a subfield of artificial intelligence."
tokens = nltk.word_tokenize(text)
print("Tokens:", tokens)
# Part-of-speech tagging
pos_tags = nltk.pos_tag(tokens)
print("POS Tags:", pos_tags)
```

2. **Machine Translation:**

Python is used to build machine translation systems that automatically translate text from one language to another. Libraries like Google Translate API, OpenNMT, and MarianMT provide tools and APIs for building machine translation models.

Example:

```
# Example of machine translation using Google Translate API
from googletrans import Translator
translator = Translator()
text = "Hello, how are you?"
translated_text = translator.translate(text, dest='fr').text
print("Translated Text:", translated_text)
```

3. **Named Entity Recognition (NER):**

Python's NLP libraries enable named entity recognition, which involves identifying and categorizing entities such as persons, organizations, locations, dates, and monetary values mentioned in text.

Example:

```
# Example of named entity recognition using spaCy
import spacy
nlp = spacy.load('en_core_web_sm')
text = "Apple Inc. is headquartered in Cupertino, California."
doc = nlp(text)
for ent in doc.ents:
print(ent.text, ent.label_)
```

4. **Sentiment Analysis:**

Python is used for sentiment analysis, which involves analyzing text to determine the sentiment expressed, such as positive, negative, or neutral. Sentiment analysis is widely used in social media monitoring, customer feedback analysis, and market research.

Example:

```
# Example of sentiment analysis using TextBlob
from textblob import TextBlob
text = "This movie is amazing!"
blob = TextBlob(text)
sentiment = blob.sentiment
print("Sentiment:", sentiment)
```

5. **Chatbots:**

Python is used to build chatbots, which are AI-powered conversational agents that interact with users through text or speech. Libraries like ChatterBot, Rasa, and Dialogflow provide tools and frameworks for building chatbots with natural language understanding capabilities.

Example:

```
# Example of a simple chatbot using ChatterBot
from chatterbot import ChatBot
chatbot = ChatBot('MyChatBot')
response = chatbot.get_response('How are you?')
print(response)
```

6. **Text Generation:**

Python is used to build text generation models that generate human-like text based on input prompts. Techniques such as recurrent neural networks (RNNs), generative adversarial networks (GANs), and transformer models are used for text generation tasks.

Example:

```
# Example of text generation using GPT-3 (OpenAI)
from openai import GPT
gpt = GPT("your-api-key")
response = gpt.submit_request("Once upon a time,")
print(response.choices[0].text.strip())
```

Python's applications in artificial intelligence and natural language processing are vast and diverse, ranging from NLP tasks like sentiment analysis and named entity recognition to building chatbots, machine translation systems, and text generation models. Its simplicity, extensive library ecosystem, and powerful frameworks make it the language of choice for AI and NLP practitioners worldwide. By leveraging Python's rich ecosystem of tools and libraries, developers can build intelligent systems that understand, generate, and interact with human language, enabling a wide range of applications across various domains and industries.

Automation and Scripting:

Python's simplicity and versatility make it ideal for automation and scripting tasks, such as system administration, batch processing, and task automation.

Python is widely used for automation and scripting tasks due to its simplicity, readability, and extensive library support

1. **Task Automation:**

    Python is used to automate repetitive tasks such as file operations, data processing, system administration, and network operations. Libraries like os, shutil, and subprocess provide tools for interacting with the file system, executing shell commands, and managing processes, enabling automation of various tasks.

Example:

```python
# Example of task automation: file operations
import os
import shutil
# Move files from one directory to another
source_dir = '/path/to/source'
destination_dir = '/path/to/destination'
files = os.listdir(source_dir)
for file in files:
shutil.move(os.path.join(source_dir, file), destination_dir)
```

2. **Web Scraping:**

Python is used for web scraping, which involves extracting data from websites. Libraries like BeautifulSoup and Scrapy provide tools for parsing HTML and XML documents, making it easy to retrieve and process data from the web.

Example:

```python
# Example of web scraping using BeautifulSoup
import requests
from bs4 import BeautifulSoup
url = 'https://www.example.com'
response = requests.get(url)
soup = BeautifulSoup(response.text, 'html.parser')
# Extract data from the webpage
data = []
for item in soup.find_all('div', class_='item'):
title = item.find('h2').text
price = item.find('span', class_='price').text
data.append({'title': title, 'price': price})
# Save data to a CSV file
import csv
with open('data.csv', 'w', newline='') as csvfile:
fieldnames = ['title', 'price']
writer = csv.DictWriter(csvfile, fieldnames=fieldnames)
```

```
writer.writeheader()
for item in data:
writer.writerow(item)
```

3. **Scripting for System Administration:**

Python is used for system administration tasks such as managing files, directories, users, permissions, and system configuration. Libraries like os, sys, and subprocess provide tools for interacting with the operating system, executing shell commands, and managing processes.

Example:

```
# Example of system administration scripting
import os
import sys
import subprocess
# Display system information
print("Operating System:", sys.platform)
print("Current Directory:", os.getcwd())
# Execute shell command
result = subprocess.run(['ls', '-l'], capture_output=True, text=True)
print("List of files:")
print(result.stdout)
```

4. **Automation of Data Processing:**

Python is used for automating data processing tasks such as data cleaning, transformation, and analysis. Libraries like pandas and NumPy provide tools for working with structured data, performing mathematical operations, and statistical analysis, enabling automation of data-related tasks.

Example:

```
# Example of data processing automation using pandas
import pandas as pd
# Load data into a pandas DataFrame
```

```
data = pd.read_csv('data.csv')
# Perform data cleaning and transformation
data['date'] = pd.to_datetime(data['date'])
data['sales'] = data['quantity'] * data['unit_price']
# Perform statistical analysis
summary_stats = data.describe()
```

5. Automation of Network Operations:

Python is used for automating network operations such as network configuration, monitoring, and troubleshooting. Libraries like paramiko and netmiko provide tools for SSH and Telnet communication, enabling automation of network tasks across multiple devices.

Example:

```
# Example of network automation using netmiko
from netmiko import ConnectHandler
# Connect to a network device
device = {
'device_type': 'cisco_ios',
'host': 'router.example.com',
'username': 'admin',
'password': 'password',
}
connection = ConnectHandler(**device)
# Execute commands on the device
output = connection.send_command('show interfaces')
print(output)
# Disconnect from the device
connection.disconnect()
```

Python's simplicity, readability, and extensive library support make it an ideal choice for automation and scripting tasks. Whether automating repetitive tasks, web scraping, system administration, data processing, or network operations, Python provides powerful tools and libraries that streamline the development process and enable developers to build efficient and robust automation solutions. By leveraging Python's rich ecosystem of libraries and tools, developers can automate a wide range of tasks across various domains and industries, improving productivity and efficiency.

4. Example: Hello World Program in Python:

Hello World program in Python

print("Hello, World!")

Python's popularity stems from its simplicity, readability, and versatility, making it suitable for a wide range of applications, from web development and data science to artificial intelligence and automation. Its rich ecosystem of libraries, expressive syntax, and extensive community support make Python an excellent choice for both beginners and experienced programmers looking to develop robust and scalable software solutions. In the following sections, we will delve deeper into Python programming, exploring its various features, libraries, and best practices for software development.

Basics of Data Structures and Algorithms:

Data structures and algorithms are fundamental concepts in computer science and programming. Understanding these concepts is essential for writing efficient and optimized code.

1. **Data Structures:**

A data structure is a way of organizing and storing data in a computer's memory so that it can be accessed and manipulated efficiently. Different data structures are suitable for different types of applications and operations. Common data structures include arrays, linked lists, stacks, queues, trees, and graphs.

Importance of Data Structures:

- Efficient data storage and retrieval
- Facilitate efficient algorithms implementation
- Enable faster search, insertion, deletion, and traversal operations

• Provide organization and structure to data

2. Algorithms:

An algorithm is a step-by-step procedure or set of rules for solving a problem or performing a computation. Algorithms operate on data structures and manipulate the data stored in them to produce desired outcomes. Algorithms can be categorized based on their time complexity, space complexity, and problem-solving approach (e.g., sorting, searching, graph traversal).

Importance of Algorithms:

• Solve problems efficiently and optimally
• Improve performance and scalability of software applications
• Provide systematic approaches to problem-solving
• Enable analysis and comparison of different solutions

Common Data Structures:

1. Arrays: A contiguous collection of elements stored in memory, accessible by index. Arrays have constant-time access but may have limitations on insertion and deletion operations.
2. Linked Lists: A collection of nodes, where each node contains data and a reference (pointer) to the next node. Linked lists support dynamic memory allocation and efficient insertion and deletion operations.
3. Stacks: A last-in, first-out (LIFO) data structure where elements are added and removed from the top (end) of the stack. Stacks are used in function call management, expression evaluation, and backtracking algorithms.
4. Queues: A first-in, first-out (FIFO) data structure where elements are added at the rear (end) and removed from the front (beginning) of the queue. Queues are used in process scheduling, task management, and breadth-first search algorithms.

5. Trees: A hierarchical data structure composed of nodes connected by edges, where each node has a parent and zero or more children. Trees are used in hierarchical data representation, binary search trees, and decision-making processes.

6. Graphs: A non-linear data structure consisting of nodes (vertices) and edges that connect pairs of nodes. Graphs are used in network modeling, shortest path algorithms, and social network analysis.

Common Algorithms:

1. Sorting Algorithms: Algorithms for arranging elements of a list in a specific order, such as bubble sort, selection sort, insertion sort, merge sort, quick sort, and heap sort.

2. Searching Algorithms: Algorithms for finding a particular element within a collection, such as linear search, binary search, depth-first search (DFS), and breadth-first search (BFS).

3. Graph Algorithms: Algorithms for traversing and manipulating graphs, such as depth-first search (DFS), breadth-first search (BFS), Dijkstra's algorithm, and minimum spanning tree algorithms (Prim's and Kruskal's algorithms).

4. Dynamic Programming: A method for solving complex problems by breaking them down into simpler subproblems and solving each subproblem only once, storing the solutions to subproblems to avoid redundant computation.

5. Recursion: A technique where a function calls itself to solve smaller instances of the same problem, typically used in problems that can be divided into smaller identical problems.

6. Greedy Algorithms: Algorithms that make locally optimal choices at each step with the hope of finding a global optimum, often used in optimization problems.

Conclusion:

Understanding the basics of data structures and algorithms is crucial for any programmer or software engineer. By mastering data structures and algorithms, developers can write efficient, scalable, and optimized code to solve complex problems and build high-performance software applications. These concepts serve as the foundation for computer science and programming and are essential for building a strong programming skill set.

Chapter 3: Understanding Machine Learning Libraries

Machine learning libraries are essential tools for implementing and deploying machine learning algorithms efficiently. These libraries provide a wide range of algorithms, tools, and utilities for various tasks such as data preprocessing, model training, evaluation, and deployment.

1. Scikit-learn:

Scikit-learn is one of the most widely used machine learning libraries in Python. It provides simple and efficient tools for data mining and data analysis, built on top of NumPy, SciPy, and matplotlib. Scikit-learn offers a wide range of supervised and unsupervised learning algorithms, including classification, regression, clustering, dimensionality reduction, and model selection.

Example:

```
# Example of using scikit-learn for classification
from sklearn.datasets import load_iris
from sklearn.model_selection import train_test_split
from sklearn.linear_model import LogisticRegression
from sklearn.metrics import accuracy_score
# Load dataset
iris = load_iris()
```

```python
X, y = iris.data, iris.target
# Split data into training and testing sets
X_train, X_test, y_train, y_test = train_test_split(X, y, test_size=0.2)
# Initialize and train model
model = LogisticRegression()
model.fit(X_train, y_train)
# Make predictions
predictions = model.predict(X_test)
# Evaluate model accuracy
accuracy = accuracy_score(y_test, predictions)
print("Accuracy:", accuracy)
```

2. TensorFlow:

TensorFlow is an open-source machine learning framework developed by Google. It provides tools for building and training deep learning models efficiently, with support for both CPU and GPU computation. TensorFlow offers high-level APIs like Keras for easy model building and deployment, as well as low-level APIs for advanced customization.

Example:

```python
# Example of using TensorFlow with Keras for building a neural network
import tensorflow as tf
from tensorflow.keras.models import Sequential
from tensorflow.keras.layers import Dense
# Build the model
model = Sequential([
Dense(64, activation='relu', input_shape=(784,)),
Dense(64, activation='relu'),
Dense(10, activation='softmax')
])
# Compile the model
model.compile(optimizer='adam',
loss='sparse_categorical_crossentropy',
metrics=['accuracy'])
```

```python
# Train the model
model.fit(X_train, y_train, epochs=5)
# Evaluate the model
loss, accuracy = model.evaluate(X_test, y_test)
print("Test Accuracy:", accuracy)
```

3. PyTorch:

PyTorch is another popular open-source machine learning framework developed by Facebook. It provides a flexible and dynamic approach to building deep learning models, with support for automatic differentiation and GPU acceleration. PyTorch is known for its ease of use and flexibility, making it a preferred choice for researchers and practitioners.

Example:

```python
# Example of using PyTorch for building a neural network
import torch
import torch.nn as nn
import torch.optim as optim
# Define the model architecture
class NeuralNetwork(nn.Module):
def __init__(self):
super(NeuralNetwork, self).__init__()
self.fc1 = nn.Linear(784, 64)
self.fc2 = nn.Linear(64, 64)
self.fc3 = nn.Linear(64, 10)
def forward(self, x):
x = torch.relu(self.fc1(x))
x = torch.relu(self.fc2(x))
x = torch.softmax(self.fc3(x), dim=1)
return x
# Initialize the model
model = NeuralNetwork()
# Define loss function and optimizer
criterion = nn.CrossEntropyLoss()
optimizer = optim.Adam(model.parameters(), lr=0.001)
```

```
# Train the model
for epoch in range(5):
for inputs, labels in train_loader:
optimizer.zero_grad()
outputs = model(inputs)
loss = criterion(outputs, labels)
loss.backward()
optimizer.step()
# Evaluate the model
correct = 0
total = 0
with torch.no_grad():
for inputs, labels in test_loader:
outputs = model(inputs)
_, predicted = torch.max(outputs.data, 1)
total += labels.size(0)
correct += (predicted == labels).sum().item()
accuracy = correct / total
print('Test Accuracy:', accuracy)
```

4. XGBoost:

XGBoost is a scalable and efficient machine learning library for gradient boosting. It provides an implementation of gradient boosting algorithms that are widely used for classification, regression, and ranking tasks. XGBoost is known for its speed, accuracy, and scalability, making it a popular choice in data science competitions and real-world applications.

Example:

```
# Example of using XGBoost for classification
import xgboost as xgb
# Define the dataset
dtrain = xgb.DMatrix(X_train, label=y_train)
dtest = xgb.DMatrix(X_test, label=y_test)
# Define parameters for XGBoost model
params = {
```

```
'objective': 'multi:softmax',
'num_class': 10,
'eval_metric': 'merror'
}
# Train the model
num_rounds = 10
model = xgb.train(params, dtrain, num_rounds)
# Make predictions
predictions = model.predict(dtest)
# Evaluate model accuracy
accuracy = accuracy_score(y_test, predictions)
print("Accuracy:", accuracy)
```

Introduction to TensorFlow:

TensorFlow is an open-source machine learning framework developed by Google. It provides tools for building and training deep learning models efficiently, with support for both CPU and GPU computation. TensorFlow is widely used in various applications such as image recognition, natural language processing, and reinforcement learning.

1. Basics of TensorFlow:

TensorFlow uses a computational graph paradigm where operations are nodes in the graph and tensors are edges that flow between nodes. The graph defines the computation to be performed, and TensorFlow optimizes and executes the graph efficiently using CPU or GPU resources.

Example:

```
import tensorflow as tf
# Define computational graph
a = tf.constant(5)
b = tf.constant(3)
c = tf.add(a, b)
# Execute the graph
```

```
with tf.Session() as sess:
result = sess.run(c)
print(result) # Output: 8
```

2. TensorFlow Operations:

TensorFlow provides a wide range of operations for mathematical computations, tensor manipulation, neural network layers, activation functions, loss functions, and optimization algorithms. These operations can be used to build complex neural network architectures and perform various machine learning tasks.

Example:

```
import tensorflow as tf
# Define placeholders for input data
X = tf.placeholder(tf.float32, shape=[None, 784])
y = tf.placeholder(tf.int64, shape=[None])
# Define neural network architecture
hidden = tf.layers.dense(X, 64, activation=tf.nn.relu)
output = tf.layers.dense(hidden, 10, activation=None)
# Define loss function and optimizer
loss = tf.losses.sparse_softmax_cross_entropy(labels=y, logits=output)
optimizer = tf.train.AdamOptimizer(learning_rate=0.001)
train_op = optimizer.minimize(loss)
```

3. TensorFlow Eager Execution:

TensorFlow also supports eager execution, which allows for immediate evaluation of operations without building a computational graph. Eager execution enables interactive debugging, intuitive API usage, and dynamic model construction.

Example:

```
import tensorflow as tf
# Enable eager execution
tf.enable_eager_execution()
# Perform immediate evaluation of operations
a = tf.constant(5)
```

```
b = tf.constant(3)
c = tf.add(a, b)
print(c) # Output: tf.Tensor(8, shape=(), dtype=int32)
```

4. TensorFlow Keras API:

TensorFlow provides the Keras API, which is a high-level neural networks API that simplifies the process of building and training deep learning models. Keras offers a user-friendly interface for defining neural network architectures, training models, and deploying them for inference.

Example:

```
import tensorflow as tf
# Build a simple neural network using Keras
model = tf.keras.Sequential([
tf.keras.layers.Dense(64, activation='relu', input_shape=(784,)),
tf.keras.layers.Dense(64, activation='relu'),
tf.keras.layers.Dense(10, activation='softmax')
])
# Compile the model
model.compile(optimizer='adam',
loss='sparse_categorical_crossentropy',
metrics=['accuracy'])
# Train the model
model.fit(X_train, y_train, epochs=5, validation_data=(X_val, y_val))
# Evaluate the model
loss, accuracy = model.evaluate(X_test, y_test)
print("Test Loss:", loss)
print("Test Accuracy:", accuracy)
```

5. TensorFlow Estimators:

TensorFlow Estimators provide a high-level API for building and training machine learning models. Estimators encapsulate the training, evaluation, prediction, and export functionalities, making it easy to create production-ready models.

Example:

```python
import tensorflow as tf
# Define feature columns
feature_columns = [tf.feature_column.numeric_column('x', shape=[784])]
# Define Estimator
estimator = tf.estimator.DNNClassifier(
feature_columns=feature_columns,
hidden_units=[64, 64],
n_classes=10,
model_dir='model'
)
# Train the Estimator
train_input_fn = tf.estimator.inputs.numpy_input_fn(
x={'x': X_train},
y=y_train,
num_epochs=None,
shuffle=True
)
estimator.train(input_fn=train_input_fn, steps=1000)
# Evaluate the Estimator
eval_input_fn = tf.estimator.inputs.numpy_input_fn(
x={'x': X_test},
y=y_test,
num_epochs=1,
shuffle=False
)
metrics = estimator.evaluate(input_fn=eval_input_fn)
print("Test Accuracy:", metrics['accuracy'])
```

TensorFlow is a powerful and flexible machine learning framework that provides tools for building and training deep learning models efficiently. Whether you're building simple neural networks or complex deep learning architectures, TensorFlow offers a wide range of features and APIs to suit your needs. By leveraging TensorFlow's capabilities, developers and researchers can build cutting-edge machine learning models and deploy them for various real-world applications.

Getting Started with PyTorch:

PyTorch is a widely used open-source machine learning library developed by Facebook's AI Research lab. It is known for its flexibility, dynamic computation graph, and ease of use. PyTorch provides tools for building and training deep learning models efficiently, making it a popular choice among researchers and practitioners.

1. Basics of PyTorch:

PyTorch uses dynamic computation graphs, allowing for flexible and intuitive model construction. It provides tensor operations similar to NumPy, but with GPU acceleration for faster computation. PyTorch supports automatic differentiation, making it easy to compute gradients for training deep learning models using gradient descent-based optimization algorithms.

Example:

```
import torch
# Create tensors
x = torch.tensor([1, 2, 3])
y = torch.tensor([4, 5, 6])
# Perform tensor operations
z = x + y
print(z) # Output: tensor([5, 7, 9])
# Automatic differentiation
x = torch.tensor([2.0], requires_grad=True)
y = x**2 + 3*x + 1
y.backward()
print(x.grad) # Output: tensor([7.])
```

2. PyTorch Tensors:

PyTorch tensors are multi-dimensional arrays that can be used to represent data for deep learning tasks. Tensors can be created from

Python lists, NumPy arrays, or generated using built-in functions. PyTorch tensors support various operations such as element-wise operations, matrix operations, and broadcasting.

Example:

```python
import torch
# Create tensors
x = torch.tensor([[1, 2], [3, 4]])
y = torch.tensor([[5, 6], [7, 8]])
# Perform tensor operations
z = torch.matmul(x, y)
print(z) # Output: tensor([[19, 22], [43, 50]])
```

3. PyTorch Modules and Neural Networks:

PyTorch provides the **torch.nn** module for building neural networks. Neural network architectures can be defined by subclassing **torch.nn.Module** and implementing the **forward** method. PyTorch also provides a wide range of built-in layers, activation functions, loss functions, and optimization algorithms for building and training neural networks.

Example:

```python
import torch
import torch.nn as nn
import torch.optim as optim
# Define neural network architecture
class NeuralNetwork(nn.Module):
def __init__(self):
super(NeuralNetwork, self).__init__()
self.fc1 = nn.Linear(784, 64)
self.fc2 = nn.Linear(64, 64)
self.fc3 = nn.Linear(64, 10)
def forward(self, x):
x = torch.relu(self.fc1(x))
x = torch.relu(self.fc2(x))
x = torch.softmax(self.fc3(x), dim=1)
```

```
return x
# Initialize the model
model = NeuralNetwork()
# Define loss function and optimizer
criterion = nn.CrossEntropyLoss()
optimizer = optim.Adam(model.parameters(), lr=0.001)
```

4. PyTorch DataLoader:

PyTorch provides the **torch.utils.data.DataLoader** class for loading and batching data efficiently. Data loaders can be used to iterate over datasets during training, validation, and testing. PyTorch also provides built-in datasets and transforms for common machine learning tasks.

Example:

```
import torch
from torch.utils.data import DataLoader, TensorDataset
# Define dataset and dataloader
X_train = torch.randn(1000, 784)
y_train = torch.randint(0, 10, (1000,))
train_dataset = TensorDataset(X_train, y_train)
train_loader = DataLoader(train_dataset, batch_size=32, shuffle=True)
```

5. PyTorch Training Loop:

PyTorch training loop typically consists of iterating over batches of data, performing forward and backward passes through the network, updating model parameters using optimization algorithms, and computing performance metrics.

Example:

```
import torch
# Iterate over batches of data
for inputs, labels in train_loader:
# Zero the gradients
optimizer.zero_grad()
# Forward pass
```

```
outputs = model(inputs)
# Compute loss
loss = criterion(outputs, labels)
# Backward pass
loss.backward()
# Update model parameters
optimizer.step()
```

PyTorch is a powerful and flexible machine learning library that provides tools for building and training deep learning models efficiently. Whether you're a beginner or an experienced researcher, PyTorch offers a user-friendly interface, dynamic computation graph, and extensive documentation to support your machine learning projects. By leveraging PyTorch's capabilities, developers and researchers can build cutting-edge deep learning models and deploy them for various real-world applications.

Exploring Scikit-learn:

Scikit-learn is a popular open-source machine learning library in Python that provides simple and efficient tools for data mining and data analysis. It is built on top of other scientific computing libraries such as NumPy, SciPy, and matplotlib, making it easy to integrate into existing Python workflows. Scikit-learn offers a wide range of supervised and unsupervised learning algorithms, as well as tools for model selection, evaluation, and preprocessing.

1. Basics of Scikit-learn:

Scikit-learn follows a consistent API design, making it easy to use and understand. It provides simple and intuitive interfaces for various machine learning tasks, allowing users to focus on solving problems rather than dealing with implementation details. Scikit-learn supports both traditional machine learning algorithms and more advanced techniques such as ensemble methods, dimensionality reduction, and clustering.

Example:

```
from sklearn.datasets import load_iris
from sklearn.model_selection import train_test_split
from sklearn.neighbors import KNeighborsClassifier
from sklearn.metrics import accuracy_score
# Load dataset
iris = load_iris()
X, y = iris.data, iris.target
# Split data into training and testing sets
X_train, X_test, y_train, y_test = train_test_split(X, y, test_size=0.2)
# Initialize and train model
model = KNeighborsClassifier()
model.fit(X_train, y_train)
# Make predictions
predictions = model.predict(X_test)
# Evaluate model accuracy
accuracy = accuracy_score(y_test, predictions)
print("Accuracy:", accuracy)
```

2. Supervised Learning Algorithms:

Scikit-learn provides a variety of supervised learning algorithms for classification, regression, and anomaly detection. These algorithms include decision trees, support vector machines (SVM), k-nearest neighbors (KNN), random forests, and gradient boosting methods. Scikit-learn also offers tools for feature selection, model evaluation, and hyperparameter tuning.

Example:

```
from sklearn.linear_model import LogisticRegression
from sklearn.datasets import load_digits
from sklearn.model_selection import train_test_split
from sklearn.metrics import accuracy_score
# Load dataset
digits = load_digits()
X, y = digits.data, digits.target
# Split data into training and testing sets
X_train, X_test, y_train, y_test = train_test_split(X, y, test_size=0.2)
```

```
# Initialize and train model
model = LogisticRegression()
model.fit(X_train, y_train)
# Make predictions
predictions = model.predict(X_test)
# Evaluate model accuracy
accuracy = accuracy_score(y_test, predictions)
print("Accuracy:", accuracy)
```

3. Unsupervised Learning Algorithms:

Scikit-learn also offers a variety of unsupervised learning algorithms for clustering, dimensionality reduction, and outlier detection. These algorithms include k-means clustering, hierarchical clustering, principal component analysis (PCA), and t-distributed stochastic neighbor embedding (t-SNE). Unsupervised learning algorithms can be used for exploratory data analysis, pattern recognition, and anomaly detection.

Example:

```
from sklearn.cluster import KMeans
from sklearn.datasets import load_iris
import matplotlib.pyplot as plt
# Load dataset
iris = load_iris()
X = iris.data
# Initialize and fit KMeans clustering model
model = KMeans(n_clusters=3)
model.fit(X)
# Visualize clusters
plt.scatter(X[:, 0], X[:, 1], c=model.labels_, cmap='viridis')
plt.xlabel('Sepal Length (cm)')
plt.ylabel('Sepal Width (cm)')
plt.title('KMeans Clustering')
plt.show()
```

4. Model Evaluation and Selection:

Scikit-learn provides tools for model evaluation and selection, including cross-validation, grid search, and performance metrics. Cross-validation techniques such as k-fold cross-validation and stratified k-fold cross-validation can be used to estimate model performance and assess generalization. Grid search can be used to tune hyperparameters and optimize model performance.

Example:

```
from sklearn.model_selection import GridSearchCV
from sklearn.ensemble import RandomForestClassifier
from sklearn.datasets import load_digits
# Load dataset
digits = load_digits()
X, y = digits.data, digits.target
# Initialize random forest classifier
model = RandomForestClassifier()
# Define hyperparameters grid for grid search
param_grid = {
'n_estimators': [10, 50, 100],
'max_depth': [None, 10, 20],
'min_samples_split': [2, 5, 10]
}
# Perform grid search with cross-validation
grid_search = GridSearchCV(model, param_grid, cv=5)
grid_search.fit(X, y)
# Get best model and its parameters
best_model = grid_search.best_estimator_
best_params = grid_search.best_params_
```

Scikit-learn is a versatile and powerful machine learning library that provides a wide range of tools and algorithms for various machine learning tasks. Whether you're a beginner or an experienced practitioner, Scikit-learn offers a user-friendly interface, extensive documentation, and robust implementation of machine learning algorithms. By leveraging Scikit-learn's capabilities, developers and data scientists can build, evaluate, and deploy machine learning models efficiently for various real-world applications.

Conclusion:

Machine learning libraries play a crucial role in implementing and deploying machine learning models efficiently. Whether you're working on traditional machine learning algorithms or deep learning models, there are various libraries available to suit your needs and preferences. By leveraging these libraries and their features, developers and data scientists can build, train, and deploy machine learning models effectively for various real-world applications.

Chapter 4: Fundamentals of Data Preprocessing

Data preprocessing is a crucial step in the machine learning pipeline that involves cleaning, transforming, and organizing raw data into a format suitable for machine learning models. Proper data preprocessing can significantly improve the performance and reliability of machine learning algorithms.

1. Handling Missing Data:

Missing data is a common issue in real-world datasets and can adversely affect the performance of machine learning models. There are several strategies for handling missing data, including:

- Removing rows or columns with missing values.
- Imputing missing values with statistical measures such as mean, median, or mode.
- Using advanced imputation techniques such as K-nearest neighbors (KNN) or predictive modeling.

Example:

```python
import pandas as pd
# Load dataset with missing values
df = pd.read_csv('data.csv')
# Drop rows with missing values
df.dropna(inplace=True)
```

```
# Impute missing values with mean
mean = df['column'].mean()
df['column'].fillna(mean, inplace=True)
```

2. Feature Scaling:

Feature scaling is the process of standardizing or normalizing the range of numerical features in the dataset. This ensures that all features contribute equally to the model and prevents features with larger scales from dominating the learning process. Common techniques for feature scaling include:

- Standardization (Z-score normalization): Scaling features to have zero mean and unit variance.
- Min-Max scaling: Scaling features to a fixed range, typically [0, 1] or [-1, 1].

Example:

```
from sklearn.preprocessing import StandardScaler, MinMaxScaler
# Standardize features
scaler = StandardScaler()
X_scaled = scaler.fit_transform(X)
# Min-Max scaling
scaler = MinMaxScaler()
X_scaled = scaler.fit_transform(X)
```

3. Encoding Categorical Variables:

Categorical variables are non-numeric variables that represent categories or groups. Machine learning models require numerical input, so categorical variables must be encoded into numerical format. Common encoding techniques include:

- One-hot encoding: Creating binary dummy variables for each category.
- Label encoding: Mapping each category to a unique integer.

Example:

```python
import pandas as pd
from sklearn.preprocessing import OneHotEncoder, LabelEncoder
# One-hot encoding
one_hot_encoder = OneHotEncoder()
X_encoded = one_hot_encoder.fit_transform(X)
# Label encoding
label_encoder = LabelEncoder()
X_encoded = label_encoder.fit_transform(X)
```

4. Handling Imbalanced Classes:

Imbalanced class distribution occurs when one class has significantly more samples than others. This can lead to biased model performance, where the model may favor the majority class. Techniques for handling imbalanced classes include:

- Resampling methods such as oversampling the minority class or undersampling the majority class.
- Using algorithmic approaches such as ensemble methods or cost-sensitive learning.

Example:

```python
from imblearn.over_sampling import RandomOverSampler
from imblearn.under_sampling import RandomUnderSampler
# Oversample minority class
oversampler = RandomOverSampler()
X_resampled, y_resampled = oversampler.fit_resample(X, y)
# Undersample majority class
undersampler = RandomUnderSampler()
X_resampled, y_resampled = undersampler.fit_resample(X, y)
```

5. Feature Engineering:

Feature engineering involves creating new features or transforming existing features to improve model performance. This can include:

- Creating polynomial features to capture non-linear relationships.
- Combining existing features to create new meaningful features.
- Transforming features using mathematical functions such as logarithm or square root.

Example:

```
import numpy as np
from sklearn.preprocessing import PolynomialFeatures
# Create polynomial features
poly = PolynomialFeatures(degree=2)
X_poly = poly.fit_transform(X)
# Log-transform feature
X_log = np.log(X)
```

Data preprocessing is a critical step in the machine learning pipeline that can significantly impact the performance and reliability of machine learning models. By understanding and applying fundamental data preprocessing techniques such as handling missing data, feature scaling, encoding categorical variables, handling imbalanced classes, and feature engineering, data scientists can ensure that their models are trained on clean, informative, and well-structured data, leading to more accurate and robust predictions.

Data Cleaning and Transformation:

Data cleaning and transformation are essential steps in the data preprocessing pipeline, aiming to ensure that the dataset is accurate, consistent, and suitable for analysis or modeling. This process involves identifying and handling inconsistencies, errors, missing values, outliers, and other anomalies in the dataset.

1. **Handling Missing Values:**

Missing values are a common occurrence in real-world datasets and can significantly impact the performance of machine learning models. Various strategies can be employed to handle missing values, including:

- **Dropping missing values:** Remove rows or columns with missing values if they are insignificant or cannot be imputed accurately.
- **Imputation:** Replace missing values with statistical measures such as mean, median, mode, or using more advanced techniques like K-nearest neighbors (KNN) or predictive modeling.

Example:

```python
import pandas as pd
# Load dataset with missing values
df = pd.read_csv('data.csv')
# Drop rows with missing values
df.dropna(inplace=True)
# Impute missing values with mean
mean = df['column'].mean()
df['column'].fillna(mean, inplace=True)
```

2. Handling Outliers:

Outliers are data points that deviate significantly from the rest of the dataset and may distort the analysis or modeling process. Outliers can be identified using statistical methods such as z-score, IQR (Interquartile Range), or domain-specific knowledge. Depending on the context, outliers can be handled by:

- **Removing outliers:** Exclude outliers from the dataset if they are erroneous or unlikely to represent the underlying distribution.
- **Transforming outliers:** Apply transformations such as log transformation to mitigate the influence of outliers on the analysis.

Example:

```
import numpy as np
# Detect outliers using z-score
z_scores = (df - df.mean()) / df.std()
outliers = (np.abs(z_scores) > 3).any(axis=1)
# Remove outliers
df = df[~outliers]
# Transform outliers with log transformation
df['column'] = np.log(df['column'])
```

3. Handling Inconsistent Data:

Inconsistent data refers to discrepancies or errors in the dataset, such as misspellings, inconsistent formatting, or conflicting information. To address inconsistent data:

- **Standardization:** Ensure consistent formatting and units across the dataset by converting text to lowercase, removing whitespace, or converting categorical variables to a standard format.
- **Data validation:** Perform data validation checks to identify and correct errors, such as validating numerical ranges, date formats, or categorical values against predefined lists.

Example:

```
# Standardize text data
df['column'] = df['column'].str.lower()
df['column'] = df['column'].str.strip()
# Data validation
# Example: Check if numerical values fall within valid range
valid_range = (0, 100)
df['column'] = df['column'].apply(lambda x: x if valid_range[0] <= x <= valid_range[1] else np.nan)
```

4. Feature Engineering:

Feature engineering involves creating new features or transforming existing features to extract more meaningful information and improve model performance. Techniques for feature engineering include:

- **Creating new features:** Combining existing features, generating polynomial features, or extracting features from text or timestamps.
- **Encoding categorical variables:** Converting categorical variables into numerical format using techniques like one-hot encoding or label encoding.

Example:

```
# Create new feature by combining existing features
df['new_feature'] = df['feature1'] + df['feature2']
# Generate polynomial features
from sklearn.preprocessing import PolynomialFeatures
poly = PolynomialFeatures(degree=2)
X_poly = poly.fit_transform(X)
# Encode categorical variables
df_encoded = pd.get_dummies(df, columns=['categorical_column'])
```

Data cleaning and transformation are fundamental steps in the data preprocessing pipeline, crucial for ensuring the quality and reliability of the dataset for subsequent analysis or modeling tasks. By employing techniques such as handling missing values, outliers, inconsistent data, and feature engineering, data scientists can prepare clean, informative, and structured datasets that enhance the performance and interpretability of machine learning models.

Feature Engineering:

Feature engineering is a critical component of the data preprocessing pipeline that involves creating new features or transforming existing features to improve the performance of machine learning models.

It aims to extract relevant information from raw data and represent it in a format that is more suitable for the learning algorithms. Effective feature engineering can lead to better model accuracy, interpretability, and generalization. Let's delve into the fundamentals of feature engineering techniques along with examples to illustrate their importance:

1. **Creating New Features:**

   Creating new features involves generating additional attributes from existing ones that capture important patterns or relationships in the data. This process can enhance the model's ability to learn complex patterns and improve its predictive performance.

   Example:

   Suppose we have a dataset containing the 'height' and 'weight' of individuals. We can create a new feature 'BMI' (Body Mass Index) by combining these two features:

   ```python
   import pandas as pd
   # Create a DataFrame
   data = {'height': [160, 175, 180, 165],
   'weight': [55, 70, 75, 60]}
   df = pd.DataFrame(data)
   # Create a new feature 'BMI'
   df['BMI'] = df['weight'] / ((df['height'] / 100) ** 2)
   print(df)
   ```

2. **Feature Transformation:**

   Feature transformation involves applying mathematical functions to the existing features to make them more suitable for modeling. Common transformations include log transformation, square root transformation, and box-cox transformation. These transformations can help stabilize variance, reduce skewness, and make the distribution of the features more Gaussian-like.

   Example:

   Suppose we have a skewed feature 'income' in our dataset. We can apply a log transformation to make its distribution more symmetrical:

```
import numpy as np
# Apply log transformation to 'income'
df['income_log'] = np.log(df['income'])
print(df)
```

3. **Encoding Categorical Variables:**

Categorical variables are non-numeric attributes that represent categories or groups. Machine learning models typically require numeric input, so categorical variables need to be encoded into a numerical format. Common encoding techniques include one-hot encoding, label encoding, and target encoding.

Example:

Suppose we have a categorical variable 'color' with three categories: 'red', 'green', and 'blue'. We can apply one-hot encoding to represent each category as a binary attribute:

```
# Apply one-hot encoding to 'color'
df_encoded = pd.get_dummies(df, columns=['color'])
print(df_encoded)
```

4. **Handling Interaction Terms:**

Interaction terms capture the combined effect of two or more features on the target variable. Including interaction terms in the model can help capture non-linear relationships and improve model performance.

Example:

Suppose we have two features 'age' and 'income'. We can create an interaction term 'age_income' by multiplying these two features together:

```
# Create an interaction term 'age_income'
df['age_income'] = df['age'] * df['income']
print(df)
```

5. **Dimensionality Reduction:**

Dimensionality reduction techniques such as Principal Component Analysis (PCA) and t-distributed Stochastic Neighbor Embedding (t-SNE) are used to reduce the number of features in the dataset while preserving as much information as possible. These techniques can help reduce overfitting, improve computational efficiency, and visualize high-dimensional data.

Example:

Suppose we have a dataset with a large number of features. We can apply PCA to reduce the dimensionality of the data:

```python
from sklearn.decomposition import PCA
# Apply PCA for dimensionality reduction
pca = PCA(n_components=2)
X_pca = pca.fit_transform(X)
print(X_pca)
```

Feature engineering plays a crucial role in the success of machine learning projects by extracting relevant information from raw data and representing it in a format that is conducive to learning algorithms. By employing techniques such as creating new features, transforming existing features, encoding categorical variables, handling interaction terms, and reducing dimensionality, data scientists can build more accurate, interpretable, and efficient machine learning models.

Handling Missing Data and Outliers:

Data preprocessing involves preparing raw data for analysis or modeling by addressing issues such as missing data and outliers. Missing data refers to the absence of values in a dataset, while outliers are data points that deviate significantly from the rest of the dataset. Both missing data and outliers can adversely affect the performance and reliability of machine learning models if not handled properly.

1. Handling Missing Data:

Missing data is a common occurrence in real-world datasets and can arise due to various reasons such as data entry errors, sensor malfunction, or human error. It is essential to address missing data before training machine learning models to prevent biased results and inaccurate predictions. Several techniques can be used to handle missing data:

- **Dropping missing values:** Remove rows or columns with missing values if they are insignificant or cannot be imputed accurately.
- **Imputation:** Replace missing values with statistical measures such as mean, median, mode, or using more advanced techniques like K-nearest neighbors (KNN) or predictive modeling.

Example:

Suppose we have a dataset containing information about students' exam scores, but some students have missing scores. We can handle missing data by imputing the missing scores with the mean score of the respective exam:

```python
import pandas as pd
# Load dataset with missing values
df = pd.read_csv('student_scores.csv')
# Impute missing scores with mean
mean_score = df['exam_score'].mean()
df['exam_score'].fillna(mean_score, inplace=True)
print(df)
```

2. Handling Outliers:

Outliers are data points that deviate significantly from the rest of the dataset and may indicate errors in data collection, measurement, or recording. Outliers can distort the statistical properties of the dataset and adversely affect the performance of machine learning models. It is essential to detect and handle outliers to ensure robust model performance. Techniques for handling outliers include:

- **Removing outliers:** Exclude outliers from the dataset if they are erroneous or unlikely to represent the underlying distribution.
- **Transforming outliers:** Apply transformations such as log transformation or winsorization to mitigate the influence of outliers on the analysis.

Example:

Suppose we have a dataset containing information about housing prices, and some houses have unusually high prices. We can handle outliers by removing houses with prices above the 99th percentile:

```
import numpy as np
# Detect outliers using z-score
z_scores = (df['price'] - df['price'].mean()) / df['price'].std()
outliers = np.abs(z_scores) > 3
# Remove outliers
df_cleaned = df[~outliers]
print(df_cleaned)
```

Conclusion:

Handling missing data and outliers is a critical step in the data pre-processing pipeline to ensure the quality and reliability of the dataset for subsequent analysis or modeling tasks. By employing techniques such as imputation, dropping missing values, removing outliers, or transforming outliers, data scientists can prepare clean, informative, and structured datasets that enhance the performance and interpretability of machine learning models.

Chapter 5: Supervised Learning Algorithms

Supervised learning is a type of machine learning where the algorithm learns from labeled data, which means each input data point is associated with a corresponding target label. The goal of supervised learning is to learn a mapping function from input variables to output variables based on the labeled training data.

1. **Linear Regression:**

   Linear regression is a simple and widely used supervised learning algorithm for regression tasks. It models the relationship between a dependent variable (target) and one or more independent variables (features) by fitting a linear equation to the observed data.

   Example: Consider a dataset containing information about houses, such as their size and price. Using linear regression, we can predict the price of a house based on its size.

```
from sklearn.linear_model import LinearRegression
# Define features and target variables
X = df[['size']] # Feature (independent variable)
y = df['price'] # Target (dependent variable)
# Initialize and train the linear regression model
model = LinearRegression()
model.fit(X, y)
```

```
# Make predictions
new_house_size = 2000
predicted_price = model.predict([[new_house_size]])
print("Predicted price:", predicted_price)
```

2. **Logistic Regression:**

Logistic regression is a supervised learning algorithm for binary classification tasks. It models the probability that a given input belongs to a particular class using the logistic function.

Example: Consider a dataset containing information about whether emails are spam or not. Using logistic regression, we can classify emails as spam or not based on features such as the presence of certain keywords.

```
from sklearn.linear_model import LogisticRegression
# Define features and target variables
X = df[['word1_count', 'word2_count', '...']] # Features
y = df['spam'] # Target variable (binary: spam or not)
# Initialize and train the logistic regression model
model = LogisticRegression()
model.fit(X, y)
# Make predictions
new_email = ['free', 'money', 'click', ...] # Features of the new email
predicted_class = model.predict([new_email])
print("Predicted class:", predicted_class)
```

3. **Decision Trees:**

Decision trees are versatile supervised learning algorithms for both classification and regression tasks. They learn a hierarchical structure of if-else decision rules from the training data to make predictions.

Example: Consider a dataset containing information about whether customers will purchase a product based on their age and income. Using a decision tree, we can predict whether a customer will make a purchase.

```
from sklearn.tree import DecisionTreeClassifier
# Define features and target variables
X = df[['age', 'income']] # Features
y = df['purchase'] # Target variable (binary: purchase or not)
# Initialize and train the decision tree model
model = DecisionTreeClassifier()
model.fit(X, y)
# Make predictions
new_customer = [35, 50000] # Features of the new customer
predicted_purchase = model.predict([new_customer])
print("Predicted purchase:", predicted_purchase)
```

4. **Support Vector Machines (SVM):**

Support Vector Machines (SVM) are powerful supervised learning algorithms for classification tasks. They find the optimal hyperplane that separates data points of different classes with the maximum margin.

Example: Consider a dataset containing information about whether patients have a particular disease based on their medical test results. Using SVM, we can classify patients as having the disease or not.

```
from sklearn.svm import SVC
# Define features and target variables
X = df[['test1', 'test2', ...]] # Features
y = df['disease'] # Target variable (binary: disease or not)
# Initialize and train the SVM model
model = SVC(kernel='linear')
model.fit(X, y)
# Make predictions
new_patient_test_results = [0.8, 0.6, ...] # Features of the new patient
predicted_disease = model.predict([new_patient_test_results])
print("Predicted disease:", predicted_disease)
```

Supervised learning algorithms play a crucial role in various machine learning tasks, including regression, binary classification, and multiclass classification. By understanding and applying these algorithms, data scientists can build predictive models that learn from labeled data to make accurate predictions on unseen data. These examples provide a glimpse into the versatility and practicality of supervised learning algorithms in real-world scenarios.

Linear Regression:

Linear regression is one of the fundamental and widely used supervised learning algorithms for regression tasks. It models the relationship between a dependent variable (target) and one or more independent variables (features) by fitting a linear equation to the observed data points. The goal of linear regression is to find the best-fitting line that minimizes the sum of the squared differences between the observed and predicted values.

1. **Understanding Linear Regression:**

   Linear regression assumes that there exists a linear relationship between the independent variables (features) and the dependent variable (target). Mathematically, the relationship can be represented as:

   $y = \beta 0 + \beta 1 x1 + \beta 2 x2 + ... + \beta n xn + \epsilon$

   Where:

   y is the dependent variable (target).

   $x1, x2, ..., xn$ are the independent variables (features).

   $\beta 0, \beta 1, \beta 2, ..., \beta n$ are the coefficients (parameters) to be estimated.

   ϵ is the error term.

   The goal is to estimate the coefficients $\beta 0, \beta 1, \beta 2, ..., \beta n$ that minimize the sum of squared residuals between the observed and predicted values.

2. **Example: Predicting House Prices with Linear Regression:**

   Consider a dataset containing information about houses, such as their size (in square feet) and price (in dollars). We want to build a linear regression model to predict the price of a house based on its size.

```
import pandas as pd
from sklearn.model_selection import train_test_split
from sklearn.linear_model import LinearRegression
from sklearn.metrics import mean_squared_error
# Load dataset
df = pd.read_csv('house_prices.csv')
# Define features (X) and target variable (y)
X = df[['size']] # Feature (independent variable)
y = df['price'] # Target (dependent variable)
# Split the dataset into training and testing sets
X_train, X_test, y_train, y_test = train_test_split(X, y,
test_size=0.2, random_state=42)
# Initialize and train the linear regression model
model = LinearRegression()
model.fit(X_train, y_train)
# Make predictions on the testing set
y_pred = model.predict(X_test)
# Evaluate model performance
mse = mean_squared_error(y_test, y_pred)
print("Mean Squared Error:", mse)
```

3. **Interpreting the Results:**

- The linear regression model learns the relationship between the size of houses and their prices.
- The coefficients $0\beta0$ and $1\beta1$ represent the intercept and slope of the regression line, respectively.
- The mean squared error (MSE) quantifies the average squared difference between the observed and predicted house prices. Lower MSE indicates better model performance.

4. **Advantages of Linear Regression:**

- Simplicity: Linear regression is simple to understand and interpret, making it suitable for introductory machine learning tasks.
- Efficiency: Linear regression models can be trained quickly, even on large datasets.
- Transparency: The linear relationship between features and the target variable can be visualized and interpreted easily.

5. Limitations of Linear Regression:

- Linearity Assumption: Linear regression assumes that the relationship between features and the target variable is linear, which may not always hold true in real-world scenarios.
- Sensitivity to Outliers: Linear regression is sensitive to outliers, which can significantly impact the model's performance.
- Limited Complexity: Linear regression cannot capture complex nonlinear relationships between features and the target variable.

Linear regression is a powerful and versatile supervised learning algorithm for regression tasks. By understanding its principles and applying it to real-world datasets, data scientists can build predictive models to make accurate predictions and gain valuable insights from their data. However, it's essential to consider the assumptions and limitations of linear regression when applying it to specific problems.

Logistic Regression:

Logistic regression is a popular and widely used supervised learning algorithm for binary classification tasks. Despite its name, logistic regression is used for classification rather than regression. It models the probability that a given input belongs to a particular class using the logistic function.

1. Understanding Logistic Regression:

Logistic regression is used to model the probability that a binary outcome variable *y* belongs to a particular class based on one or more predictor variables $1,2,...,x1,x2,...,xn$. The logistic regression model applies the logistic (sigmoid) function to the linear combination of the predictor variables:

$P(y=1|\mathbf{x})=1+e-(\beta0+\beta1x1+\beta2x2+...+\beta nxn)1$

Where:

- $P(y=1|\mathbf{x})$ is the probability that the outcome variable ❖*y* is equal to 1 (belongs to the positive class) given the predictor variables **x**.
- $\beta0,\beta1,\beta2,...,\beta n$ are the coefficients (parameters) to be estimated.
- *e* is the base of the natural logarithm.

The logistic function maps the linear combination of predictor variables to a value between 0 and 1, representing the probability of belonging to the positive class.

2. Example: Predicting Spam Emails with Logistic Regression:

Consider a dataset containing information about emails, such as the frequency of certain words and whether they are spam or not. We want to build a logistic regression model to classify emails as spam or not based on their features.

```
import pandas as pd
from sklearn.model_selection import train_test_split
from sklearn.linear_model import LogisticRegression
from sklearn.metrics import accuracy_score, classification_report
# Load dataset
df = pd.read_csv('spam_emails.csv')
# Define features (X) and target variable (y)
X = df[['word1_count', 'word2_count', ...]] # Features
y = df['spam'] # Target variable (binary: spam or not)
# Split the dataset into training and testing sets
```

```
X_train, X_test, y_train, y_test = train_test_split(X, y, test_size=0.2,
random_state=42)
    # Initialize and train the logistic regression model
    model = LogisticRegression()
    model.fit(X_train, y_train)
    # Make predictions on the testing set
    y_pred = model.predict(X_test)
    # Evaluate model performance
    accuracy = accuracy_score(y_test, y_pred)
    report = classification_report(y_test, y_pred)
    print("Accuracy:", accuracy)
    print("Classification Report:\n", report)
```

3. Interpreting the Results:

- The logistic regression model learns the relationship between the features (word frequencies) and the probability of an email being spam.
- The coefficients $\beta 0, \beta 1, \beta 2, ..., \beta n$ represent the impact of each feature on the log-odds of the email being spam.
- The accuracy score and classification report provide insights into the model's performance in classifying emails as spam or not.

4. Advantages of Logistic Regression:

- Simple and interpretable: Logistic regression models are easy to understand and interpret, making them suitable for introductory machine learning tasks.
- Efficient: Logistic regression models can be trained quickly, even on large datasets.
- Probabilistic interpretation: Logistic regression provides probabilistic predictions, allowing for uncertainty estimation.

5. Limitations of Logistic Regression:

- Limited to binary classification: Logistic regression is primarily used for binary classification tasks and cannot directly handle multi-class classification problems.
- Linear decision boundary: Logistic regression assumes a linear decision boundary between classes, which may not capture complex relationships in the data.
- Sensitivity to outliers: Logistic regression is sensitive to outliers, which can affect model performance.

Logistic regression is a versatile and widely used supervised learning algorithm for binary classification tasks. By understanding its principles and applying it to real-world datasets, data scientists can build predictive models to classify data into two categories based on their features. However, it's essential to consider the assumptions and limitations of logistic regression when applying it to specific problems.

Decision Trees and Random Forests:

Decision trees and random forests are powerful supervised learning algorithms used for both classification and regression tasks. They are known for their simplicity, interpretability, and ability to handle complex relationships in the data.

1. **Decision Trees:**

   Decision trees are hierarchical structures consisting of nodes that represent decisions based on feature values. Each internal node represents a decision based on a feature, and each leaf node represents a class label or a regression value. Decision trees recursively split the dataset into subsets based on the value of a feature that maximizes the information gain or minimizes impurity.

   Example: Predicting Titanic Survivors with Decision Trees:

Consider a dataset containing information about Titanic passengers, such as age, gender, and ticket class. We want to build a decision tree model to predict whether a passenger survived the Titanic disaster.

```python
import pandas as pd
from sklearn.model_selection import train_test_split
from sklearn.tree import DecisionTreeClassifier
from sklearn.metrics import accuracy_score, classification_report
# Load dataset
df = pd.read_csv('titanic.csv')
# Preprocess data (handle missing values, encode categorical variables, etc.)
# Define features (X) and target variable (y)
X = df[['Age', 'Sex', 'Pclass']] # Features
y = df['Survived'] # Target variable (binary: 0 for not survived, 1 for survived)
# Split the dataset into training and testing sets
X_train, X_test, y_train, y_test = train_test_split(X, y, test_size=0.2, random_state=42)
# Initialize and train the decision tree model
model = DecisionTreeClassifier()
model.fit(X_train, y_train)
# Make predictions on the testing set
y_pred = model.predict(X_test)
# Evaluate model performance
accuracy = accuracy_score(y_test, y_pred)
report = classification_report(y_test, y_pred)
print("Accuracy:", accuracy)
print("Classification Report:\n", report)
```

2. **Random Forests:**

Random forests are an ensemble learning method that combines multiple decision trees to improve predictive performance and reduce overfitting. Random forests train each decision tree on a random subset of the training data and randomly select a subset of features for each split. The final prediction is made by averaging the predictions of all decision trees (for regression tasks) or using a majority vote (for classification tasks).

Example: Predicting Iris Species with Random Forests:

Consider a dataset containing information about iris flowers, such as sepal length, sepal width, petal length, and petal width. We want to build a random forest model to classify iris flowers into three species: setosa, versicolor, and virginica.

```python
import pandas as pd
from sklearn.model_selection import train_test_split
from sklearn.ensemble import RandomForestClassifier
from sklearn.metrics import accuracy_score, classification_report
# Load dataset
df = pd.read_csv('iris.csv')
# Define features (X) and target variable (y)
X = df[['SepalLengthCm', 'SepalWidthCm', 'PetalLengthCm', 'PetalWidthCm']] # Features
y = df['Species'] # Target variable (multi-class: setosa, versicolor, virginica)
# Split the dataset into training and testing sets
X_train, X_test, y_train, y_test = train_test_split(X, y, test_size=0.2, random_state=42)
# Initialize and train the random forest model
model = RandomForestClassifier()
model.fit(X_train, y_train)
# Make predictions on the testing set
y_pred = model.predict(X_test)
# Evaluate model performance
accuracy = accuracy_score(y_test, y_pred)
report = classification_report(y_test, y_pred)
print("Accuracy:", accuracy)
print("Classification Report:\n", report)
```

Decision trees and random forests are powerful supervised learning algorithms used for both classification and regression tasks. By understanding their principles and applying them to real-world datasets, data scientists can build predictive models to classify data into multiple categories or predict continuous outcomes. However, it's essential to tune the hyperparameters of decision trees and random forests to achieve optimal performance and prevent overfitting.

Support Vector Machines:

Support Vector Machines (SVM) are powerful supervised learning algorithms used for classification and regression tasks. SVMs are known for their effectiveness in handling high-dimensional data and finding the optimal hyperplane that best separates data points of different classes.

1. **Understanding Support Vector Machines:**

   Support Vector Machines aim to find the hyperplane that maximizes the margin between the classes in the feature space. The hyperplane is chosen such that it separates the data points of different classes with the maximum margin, minimizing the classification error. In cases where the data is not linearly separable, SVMs use the kernel trick to transform the data into a higher-dimensional space where linear separation is possible.

   Example: Binary Classification with Linear SVM

   Consider a dataset containing two classes of data points, represented as red and blue dots in a two-dimensional feature space. We want to build a Support Vector Machine model to classify these data points into their respective classes.

```python
import numpy as np
import matplotlib.pyplot as plt
from sklearn import svm
# Generate synthetic data
np.random.seed(0)
```

```
X = np.r_[np.random.randn(20, 2) - [2, 2], np.random.randn(20,
2) + [2, 2]]
y = [-1] * 20 + [1] * 20
# Fit SVM model
model = svm.SVC(kernel='linear')
model.fit(X, y)
# Plot decision boundary
plt.scatter(X[:, 0], X[:, 1], c=y, cmap=plt.cm.Paired)
ax = plt.gca()
xlim = ax.get_xlim()
ylim = ax.get_ylim()
# Create grid to evaluate model
xx, yy = np.meshgrid(np.linspace(xlim[0], xlim[1], 50), np.lin-
space(ylim[0], ylim[1], 50))
Z = model.decision_function(np.c_[xx.ravel(), yy.ravel()])
# Plot decision boundary and margins
Z = Z.reshape(xx.shape)
ax.contour(xx, yy, Z, colors='k', levels=[-1, 0, 1], alpha=0.5,
linestyles=['--', '-', '--'])
plt.show()
```

2. **Kernel Trick and Non-linear SVM:**

In cases where the data is not linearly separable, SVMs use the kernel trick to transform the data into a higher-dimensional space where linear separation is possible. Commonly used kernels include polynomial, radial basis function (RBF), and sigmoid kernels.

Example: Non-linear SVM with RBF Kernel

Consider a dataset containing two classes of data points that are not linearly separable. We can use an SVM with an RBF kernel to classify these data points into their respective classes.

```
# Generate synthetic data
np.random.seed(0)
X = np.random.randn(100, 2)
y = np.logical_xor(X[:, 0] > 0, X[:, 1] > 0)
```

```
# Fit SVM model with RBF kernel
model = svm.SVC(kernel='rbf', gamma=0.1)
model.fit(X, y)
# Plot decision boundary
plt.scatter(X[:, 0], X[:, 1], c=y, cmap=plt.cm.Paired)
ax = plt.gca()
xlim = ax.get_xlim()
ylim = ax.get_ylim()
# Create grid to evaluate model
xx, yy = np.meshgrid(np.linspace(xlim[0], xlim[1], 50), np.linspace(ylim[0], ylim[1], 50))
Z = model.decision_function(np.c_[xx.ravel(), yy.ravel()])
# Plot decision boundary and margins
Z = Z.reshape(xx.shape)
ax.contour(xx, yy, Z, colors='k', levels=[-1, 0, 1], alpha=0.5, linestyles=['--', '-', '--'])
plt.show()
```

3. **Application of SVM:**

Support Vector Machines are widely used in various fields, including:

- Text classification
- Image classification
- Handwriting recognition
- Bioinformatics
- Financial forecasting
- Medical diagnosis

Support Vector Machines are powerful supervised learning algorithms used for classification and regression tasks. By understanding their principles and applying them to real-world datasets, data scientists can build predictive models to classify data points into multiple categories or predict continuous outcomes. SVMs are particularly effective in handling high-dimensional data and finding the optimal hyperplane that separates data points of different classes.

Naive Bayes Classifier:

The Naive Bayes classifier is a simple yet powerful supervised learning algorithm based on Bayes' theorem with an assumption of independence between features. Despite its simplicity, Naive Bayes is known for its effectiveness in classification tasks, especially in text classification and spam filtering.

1. Understanding Naive Bayes Classifier:

The Naive Bayes classifier is based on Bayes' theorem, which states:

$$P(y|X) = P(X)P(X|y) \cdot P(y)$$

Where:

- $P(y|X)$ is the probability of class y given the features X.
- $P(X|y)$ is the likelihood of features X given class y.
- $P(y)$ is the prior probability of class y.
- $P(X)$ is the probability of features X.

The "naive" assumption in Naive Bayes is that the features are conditionally independent given the class, meaning that the presence of a particular feature in a class is independent of the presence of other features.

Example: Text Classification with Naive Bayes:

Consider a dataset containing text documents classified into different categories (e.g., sports, politics, technology). We want to build a Naive Bayes classifier to classify new documents into their respective categories.

```
import pandas as pd
from sklearn.model_selection import train_test_split
```

```
from sklearn.feature_extraction.text import CountVectorizer
from sklearn.naive_bayes import MultinomialNB
from sklearn.metrics import accuracy_score, classification_report
# Load dataset
df = pd.read_csv('text_data.csv')
# Preprocess text data and split into features and target variable
X = df['text'] # Features (text data)
y = df['category'] # Target variable (categories)
# Split the dataset into training and testing sets
X_train, X_test, y_train, y_test = train_test_split(X, y, test_size=0.2,
random_state=42)
# Vectorize text data using CountVectorizer
vectorizer = CountVectorizer()
X_train_vect = vectorizer.fit_transform(X_train)
X_test_vect = vectorizer.transform(X_test)
# Initialize and train the Naive Bayes classifier
model = MultinomialNB()
model.fit(X_train_vect, y_train)
# Make predictions on the testing set
y_pred = model.predict(X_test_vect)
# Evaluate model performance
accuracy = accuracy_score(y_test, y_pred)
report = classification_report(y_test, y_pred)
print("Accuracy:", accuracy)
print("Classification Report:\n", report)
```

2. Types of Naive Bayes Classifiers:

- **Multinomial Naive Bayes:** Suitable for text classification tasks where features represent word counts or term frequency-inverse document frequency (TF-IDF).
- **Gaussian Naive Bayes:** Suitable for continuous features with a Gaussian (normal) distribution.

- **Bernoulli Naive Bayes:** Suitable for binary or Boolean features (e.g., presence or absence of a feature).

3. Advantages of Naive Bayes Classifier:

- **Efficiency:** Naive Bayes is computationally efficient and scales well with large datasets.
- **Simplicity:** Naive Bayes is easy to implement and understand, making it suitable for introductory machine learning tasks.
- **Robustness:** Naive Bayes performs well even with small training datasets and is relatively resistant to overfitting.

4. Limitations of Naive Bayes Classifier:

- **Independence Assumption:** The assumption of feature independence may not hold true in real-world datasets, leading to suboptimal performance.
- **Zero Frequency:** If a category in the test dataset contains a feature that was not observed in the training dataset, Naive Bayes assigns a zero probability to that category, leading to incorrect predictions.

Conclusion:

The Naive Bayes classifier is a simple yet effective supervised learning algorithm widely used in text classification, spam filtering, and other classification tasks. By understanding its principles and applying it to real-world datasets, data scientists can build accurate predictive models to classify data into multiple categories based on their features. Despite its simplicity and the "naive" assumption, Naive Bayes often performs well in practice and serves as a valuable tool in the machine learning toolbox.

Chapter 6: Unsupervised Learning Algorithms

Unsupervised learning is a branch of machine learning where the model is trained on unlabeled data without any predefined outputs. The goal of unsupervised learning is to discover hidden patterns, structures, or relationships within the data. Unsupervised learning algorithms can be broadly categorized into clustering, dimensionality reduction, and association rule mining. In this comprehensive overview, we will delve into these categories, discuss popular unsupervised learning algorithms, and provide examples to illustrate their application and functionality.

1. **Clustering Algorithms:**

   Clustering algorithms group similar data points together based on their features. The aim is to partition the data into clusters, where data points within the same cluster are more similar to each other than to those in other clusters. Common clustering algorithms include K-means clustering, hierarchical clustering, and DBSCAN.

   Example: K-means Clustering

   Consider a dataset containing information about customers' spending habits. We want to group customers into distinct clusters based on their purchasing behavior.

   from sklearn.cluster import KMeans

   import matplotlib.pyplot as plt

```
import seaborn as sns
import pandas as pd
# Load dataset
data = pd.read_csv('customer_data.csv')
# Perform K-means clustering
kmeans = KMeans(n_clusters=3)
kmeans.fit(data)
# Visualize clusters
plt.scatter(data['Spending Score'], data['Annual Income'],
c=kmeans.labels_, cmap='viridis')
plt.xlabel('Spending Score')
plt.ylabel('Annual Income')
plt.title('K-means Clustering')
plt.show()
```

2. **Dimensionality Reduction Algorithms:**

Dimensionality reduction techniques aim to reduce the number of features in a dataset while preserving its essential information. These techniques are particularly useful for visualizing high-dimensional data and speeding up subsequent machine learning tasks. Common dimensionality reduction algorithms include Principal Component Analysis (PCA), t-distributed Stochastic Neighbor Embedding (t-SNE), and Singular Value Decomposition (SVD).

Example: Principal Component Analysis (PCA)

Consider a dataset containing images of handwritten digits. We want to reduce the dimensionality of the dataset for visualization purposes.

```
from sklearn.decomposition import PCA
import matplotlib.pyplot as plt
from sklearn.datasets import load_digits
# Load dataset
digits = load_digits()
# Apply PCA for dimensionality reduction
pca = PCA(n_components=2)
```

```
X_pca = pca.fit_transform(digits.data)
# Visualize reduced dimensionality data
plt.scatter(X_pca[:, 0], X_pca[:, 1], c=digits.target, cmap='viridis')
plt.xlabel('Principal Component 1')
plt.ylabel('Principal Component 2')
plt.title('PCA Dimensionality Reduction')
plt.show()
```

3. **Association Rule Mining:**

Association rule mining is used to discover interesting relationships or associations among variables in large datasets. It identifies frequent patterns, correlations, or co-occurrences between items in transactional data. A popular algorithm for association rule mining is the Apriori algorithm.

Example: Market Basket Analysis with Apriori Algorithm

Consider a dataset containing transactions from a grocery store. We want to identify frequently co-occurring items in customers' baskets.

```
from mlxtend.frequent_patterns import apriori
from mlxtend.frequent_patterns import association_rules
import pandas as pd
# Load dataset
data = pd.read_csv('grocery_transactions.csv')
# Perform Apriori algorithm
frequent_itemsets = apriori(data, min_support=0.05, use_col-
names=True)
rules = association_rules(frequent_itemsets, metric='lift',
min_threshold=1)
# Display association rules
print(rules)
```

Unsupervised learning algorithms play a crucial role in exploratory data analysis, pattern recognition, and knowledge discovery from unlabeled data. By applying clustering, dimensionality reduction, and association rule mining techniques, data scientists can gain insights into the underlying structure of the data, identify meaningful patterns, and make informed decisions. However, it's essential to choose the appropriate unsupervised learning algorithm based on the characteristics of the dataset and the specific problem domain.

K-Means Clustering:

K-Means clustering is a popular unsupervised learning algorithm used for partitioning data into distinct clusters based on their features. It aims to group similar data points together and separate different groups based on similarity, without any prior knowledge of class labels.

1. **Understanding K-Means Clustering:**

K-Means clustering works by iteratively assigning data points to the nearest centroid and updating the centroids based on the mean of the points assigned to each cluster. The algorithm proceeds as follows:

1. Initialize K centroids randomly in the feature space.
2. Assign each data point to the nearest centroid, forming K clusters.
3. Update the centroids by computing the mean of the data points in each cluster.
4. Repeat steps 2 and 3 until convergence, i.e., until the centroids no longer change significantly or a maximum number of iterations is reached.

Example: K-Means Clustering for Customer Segmentation

Consider a dataset containing information about customers' annual income and spending score. We want to segment customers into distinct groups based on their purchasing behavior.

```
import pandas as pd
import matplotlib.pyplot as plt
from sklearn.cluster import KMeans
# Load dataset
```

```
data = pd.read_csv('customer_data.csv')
# Select features
X = data[['Annual Income', 'Spending Score']]
# Initialize K-Means model
kmeans = KMeans(n_clusters=3, random_state=42)
# Fit K-Means model to data
kmeans.fit(X)
# Assign clusters to data points
data['Cluster'] = kmeans.labels_
# Visualize clusters
plt.scatter(data['Annual Income'], data['Spending Score'],
c=data['Cluster'], cmap='viridis')
plt.xlabel('Annual Income')
plt.ylabel('Spending Score')
plt.title('K-Means Clustering for Customer Segmentation')
plt.show()
```

2. Determining the Number of Clusters (K):

Choosing the appropriate number of clusters (K) is crucial for the effectiveness of K-Means clustering. Several methods, such as the Elbow Method and Silhouette Score, can be used to determine the optimal number of clusters.

Example: Using the Elbow Method to Determine K

```
# Calculate inertia (within-cluster sum of squares) for different values of K
inertia = []
for k in range(1, 11):
kmeans = KMeans(n_clusters=k, random_state=42)
kmeans.fit(X)
inertia.append(kmeans.inertia_)
# Plot inertia vs. number of clusters
plt.plot(range(1, 11), inertia, marker='o')
plt.xlabel('Number of Clusters (K)')
plt.ylabel('Inertia')
plt.title('Elbow Method for Optimal K')
```

plt.show()

3. Advantages of K-Means Clustering:

- **Simplicity:** K-Means is easy to implement and understand, making it suitable for large datasets and real-world applications.
- **Scalability:** K-Means can handle large datasets efficiently due to its computational efficiency.
- **Versatility:** K-Means can be applied to various types of data and is not restricted to specific domains.

4. Limitations of K-Means Clustering:

- **Sensitivity to Initialization:** K-Means clustering is sensitive to the initial placement of centroids, which can lead to different results for different initializations.
- **Assumption of Spherical Clusters:** K-Means assumes that clusters are spherical and isotropic, which may not hold true for all datasets.
- **Deterministic Nature:** K-Means always converges to a local optimum, and the final clustering solution depends on the initial centroids and random seed.

K-Means clustering is a versatile and widely used unsupervised learning algorithm for partitioning data into distinct clusters. By understanding its principles and applying it to real-world datasets, data scientists can gain insights into the underlying structure of the data, identify meaningful patterns, and make informed decisions. However, it's essential to choose the appropriate number of clusters and consider the limitations of K-Means when applying it to specific problems.

Hierarchical Clustering:

Hierarchical clustering is a versatile unsupervised learning algorithm used for grouping similar data points into clusters based on their features. Unlike K-Means clustering, hierarchical clustering does not require specifying the number of clusters beforehand. Instead, it creates a hierarchical tree-like structure called a dendrogram, which captures the nested relationships between clusters.

1. **Understanding Hierarchical Clustering:**

Hierarchical clustering builds a hierarchy of clusters by recursively merging or splitting clusters based on their similarity. There are two main approaches to hierarchical clustering:

- **Agglomerative Hierarchical Clustering:** It starts with each data point as a separate cluster and iteratively merges the closest pairs of clusters until only one cluster remains.
- **Divisive Hierarchical Clustering:** It starts with all data points in one cluster and recursively splits clusters into smaller clusters until each data point is in its own cluster.

Example: Agglomerative Hierarchical Clustering for Customer Segmentation

Consider a dataset containing information about customers' annual income and spending score. We want to segment customers into distinct groups based on their purchasing behavior using agglomerative hierarchical clustering.

```
import pandas as pd
import matplotlib.pyplot as plt
import scipy.cluster.hierarchy as sch
# Load dataset
data = pd.read_csv('customer_data.csv')
# Select features
```

```python
X = data[['Annual Income', 'Spending Score']]
# Perform hierarchical clustering
dendrogram = sch.dendrogram(sch.linkage(X, method='ward'))
plt.title('Dendrogram')
plt.xlabel('Customers')
plt.ylabel('Euclidean Distance')
plt.show()
```

2. Determining the Number of Clusters:

The dendrogram visually represents the hierarchical structure of clusters and helps determine the optimal number of clusters. We can use methods like cutting the dendrogram at a certain height or using the Elbow Method to identify the appropriate number of clusters.

Example: Cutting the Dendrogram

```python
# Perform hierarchical clustering with optimal number of clusters
from sklearn.cluster import AgglomerativeClustering
# Initialize hierarchical clustering model
hc = AgglomerativeClustering(n_clusters=5, affinity='euclidean', linkage='ward')
# Fit model to data and predict clusters
y_hc = hc.fit_predict(X)
```

3. Advantages of Hierarchical Clustering:

- **No Need for Predefined Number of Clusters:** Hierarchical clustering does not require specifying the number of clusters beforehand, making it suitable for exploratory data analysis.
- **Interpretability:** The dendrogram provides a visual representation of the clustering hierarchy, making it easy to interpret and understand the relationships between clusters.
- **Flexibility:** Hierarchical clustering can accommodate different distance metrics and linkage criteria, allowing users to tailor the clustering process to their specific needs.

4. Limitations of Hierarchical Clustering:

- **Computational Complexity:** Hierarchical clustering can be computationally intensive, especially for large datasets, as it requires computing pairwise distances between all data points.
- **Difficulty in Handling Large Datasets:** The memory and computational requirements of hierarchical clustering can make it challenging to apply to large datasets with thousands or millions of data points.
- **Sensitivity to Distance Metric and Linkage Criteria:** The choice of distance metric and linkage criterion can significantly impact the resulting clusters, and there is no one-size-fits-all approach.

Hierarchical clustering is a powerful unsupervised learning algorithm used for grouping similar data points into clusters based on their features. By understanding its principles and applying it to real-world datasets, data scientists can gain insights into the underlying structure of the data, identify meaningful patterns, and make informed decisions. However, it's essential to consider the computational complexity and sensitivity to parameters when applying hierarchical clustering to specific problems.

Principal Component Analysis (PCA):

Principal Component Analysis (PCA) is a fundamental unsupervised learning technique used for dimensionality reduction and data visualization. PCA aims to transform high-dimensional data into a lower-dimensional space while preserving most of the variance in the data.

1. **Understanding Principal Component Analysis:**
   PCA is based on the concept of finding the orthogonal axes (principal components) along which the data varies the most. The first principal component captures the direction of maximum variance in the data, followed by subsequent components

that capture orthogonal directions of decreasing variance. By projecting data points onto the principal components, PCA reduces the dimensionality of the data while retaining most of its information.

Example: Dimensionality Reduction with PCA

Consider a dataset containing high-dimensional data points. We want to reduce the dimensionality of the dataset using PCA while preserving most of the variance in the data.

```python
import numpy as np
import matplotlib.pyplot as plt
from sklearn.datasets import load_digits
from sklearn.decomposition import PCA
# Load dataset
digits = load_digits()
X = digits.data
y = digits.target
# Apply PCA for dimensionality reduction
pca = PCA(n_components=2)
X_pca = pca.fit_transform(X)
# Visualize reduced dimensionality data
plt.scatter(X_pca[:, 0], X_pca[:, 1], c=y, cmap='viridis')
plt.xlabel('Principal Component 1')
plt.ylabel('Principal Component 2')
plt.title('PCA Dimensionality Reduction')
plt.colorbar(label='Digit Label')
plt.show()
```

2. **Applications of Principal Component Analysis:**

- **Dimensionality Reduction:** PCA is commonly used to reduce the dimensionality of high-dimensional data while retaining most of its information. This facilitates visualization, data compression, and computational efficiency in subsequent machine learning tasks.

- **Data Visualization:** PCA can be used to visualize high-dimensional data in a lower-dimensional space, enabling exploratory data analysis and pattern recognition.
- **Noise Reduction:** PCA can help remove noise and redundant information from datasets, leading to cleaner and more interpretable data representations.
- **Feature Extraction:** PCA can be used to extract informative features from complex datasets, enabling more effective machine learning models.

3. Advantages of Principal Component Analysis:

- **Dimensionality Reduction:** PCA reduces the dimensionality of data while preserving most of its information, making it suitable for handling high-dimensional datasets.
- **Computational Efficiency:** PCA is computationally efficient and scalable to large datasets, making it applicable to real-world problems.
- **Interpretability:** PCA provides a clear interpretation of the principal components, allowing users to understand the underlying structure of the data.

4. Limitations of Principal Component Analysis:

- **Linearity Assumption:** PCA assumes that the underlying structure of the data is linear, which may not hold true for all datasets.
- **Loss of Interpretability:** While PCA reduces the dimensionality of data, it may lead to a loss of interpretability, as the transformed features may not have a direct physical or semantic meaning.

- **Sensitive to Scaling:** PCA is sensitive to the scale of the features, and standardization or normalization may be necessary to ensure optimal performance.

Principal Component Analysis (PCA) is a powerful unsupervised learning technique used for dimensionality reduction, data visualization, and feature extraction. By understanding its principles and applying it to real-world datasets, data scientists can gain insights into the underlying structure of the data, identify meaningful patterns, and make informed decisions. However, it's essential to consider the assumptions and limitations of PCA when applying it to specific problems.

t-Distributed Stochastic Neighbor Embedding (t-SNE):

t-Distributed Stochastic Neighbor Embedding (t-SNE) is a powerful unsupervised learning technique used for visualizing high-dimensional data in a lower-dimensional space. Unlike traditional dimensionality reduction techniques like PCA, t-SNE focuses on preserving local structures and capturing non-linear relationships in the data.

1. **Understanding t-Distributed Stochastic Neighbor Embedding (t-SNE):**

   t-SNE is based on the idea of representing each high-dimensional data point as a low-dimensional point in such a way that similar data points are modeled by nearby points and dissimilar data points are modeled by distant points. It accomplishes this by defining a probability distribution over pairs of high-dimensional data points and a probability distribution over pairs of low-dimensional points. It minimizes the Kullback-Leibler divergence between these two distributions, effectively preserving local structures and capturing non-linear relationships in the data.

Example: Visualizing High-Dimensional Data with t-SNE

Consider a dataset containing high-dimensional data points. We want to visualize the data in a lower-dimensional space using t-SNE.

```python
import numpy as np
import matplotlib.pyplot as plt
from sklearn.datasets import load_digits
from sklearn.manifold import TSNE
# Load dataset
digits = load_digits()
X = digits.data
y = digits.target
# Apply t-SNE for dimensionality reduction
tsne = TSNE(n_components=2, random_state=42)
X_tsne = tsne.fit_transform(X)
# Visualize reduced dimensionality data
plt.scatter(X_tsne[:, 0], X_tsne[:, 1], c=y, cmap='viridis')
plt.xlabel('t-SNE Dimension 1')
plt.ylabel('t-SNE Dimension 2')
plt.title('t-SNE Visualization of High-Dimensional Data')
plt.colorbar(label='Digit Label')
plt.show()
```

2. **Applications of t-SNE:**

- **Data Visualization:** t-SNE is primarily used for visualizing high-dimensional data in a lower-dimensional space, enabling exploratory data analysis, pattern recognition, and cluster identification.

- **Feature Extraction:** t-SNE can be used to extract informative features from complex datasets, facilitating subsequent machine learning tasks.

- **Dimensionality Reduction:** While t-SNE is not typically used for dimensionality reduction in the traditional sense, it can effectively reduce the dimensionality of data for visualization purposes.

3. Advantages of t-SNE:

- **Preservation of Local Structures:** t-SNE preserves local structures and captures non-linear relationships in the data, making it suitable for visualizing complex datasets.
- **Robustness to Noise:** t-SNE is robust to noise and outliers in the data, allowing it to handle noisy datasets effectively.
- **Flexibility:** t-SNE can be applied to various types of data and is not restricted to specific domains, making it widely applicable in practice.

4. Limitations of t-SNE:

- **Computational Complexity:** t-SNE can be computationally expensive, especially for large datasets, due to its optimization process and iterative nature.
- **Loss of Global Structure:** While t-SNE preserves local structures well, it may not preserve global structures effectively, leading to distortions in the overall layout of the data.
- **Sensitivity to Hyperparameters:** t-SNE has several hyperparameters, such as the perplexity parameter, which can significantly impact the resulting visualization and require careful tuning.

Conclusion:

t-Distributed Stochastic Neighbor Embedding (t-SNE) is a powerful unsupervised learning technique used for visualizing high-dimensional data in a lower-dimensional space. By understanding its principles and applying it to real-world datasets, data scientists can gain insights into the underlying structure of the data, identify meaningful patterns, and make informed decisions. However, it's essential to consider the computational complexity and sensitivity to hyperparameters when applying t-SNE to specific problems.

Chapter 7: Deep Learning Basics

Deep learning is a subset of machine learning that focuses on training artificial neural networks with multiple layers (hence the term "deep") to learn hierarchical representations of data. In this comprehensive overview, we will delve into the fundamental concepts of deep learning, including neural networks, activation functions, loss functions, optimization algorithms, and regularization techniques.

1. **Neural Networks:**

   Neural networks are the building blocks of deep learning models. They consist of interconnected nodes organized into layers. The input layer receives raw data, while the output layer produces the model's predictions. Intermediate layers, called hidden layers, perform transformations on the input data.

2. **Activation Functions:**

Activation functions introduce non-linearity into neural networks, allowing them to model complex relationships in data. Common activation functions include:

- **Sigmoid:** Maps input values to the range [0, 1], suitable for binary classification tasks.

- **ReLU (Rectified Linear Unit):** Returns the input if it is positive, otherwise returns zero, addressing the vanishing gradient problem and accelerating convergence in training.
- **Tanh (Hyperbolic Tangent):** Similar to the sigmoid function but maps input values to the range [-1, 1].

3. Loss Functions:

Loss functions measure the difference between the predicted output of a model and the actual target values. The choice of loss function depends on the nature of the problem, such as classification or regression tasks. Common loss functions include:

- **Mean Squared Error (MSE):** Suitable for regression tasks, computes the average squared difference between predicted and actual values.
- **Binary Cross-Entropy Loss:** Used for binary classification tasks, measures the difference between predicted probabilities and true binary labels.
- **Categorical Cross-Entropy Loss:** Applied to multi-class classification tasks, measures the difference between predicted class probabilities and true class labels.

4. Optimization Algorithms:

Optimization algorithms are used to adjust the parameters of a neural network during training to minimize the loss function. Popular optimization algorithms include:

- **Stochastic Gradient Descent (SGD):** Updates model parameters based on the gradient of the loss function with respect to each parameter.
- **Adam:** An adaptive optimization algorithm that combines ideas from RMSProp and Momentum, providing fast convergence and robustness to hyperparameters.

5. Regularization Techniques:

Regularization techniques prevent overfitting by imposing constraints on the complexity of the model. Common regularization techniques include:

- **L1 and L2 Regularization:** Add penalties to the loss function based on the magnitudes of the model parameters to discourage large parameter values.
- **Dropout:** Randomly sets a fraction of input units to zero during training, preventing units from co-adapting and acting as "regularization by noise."

Introduction to Neural Networks:

Neural networks are the foundational building blocks of deep learning, designed to mimic the structure and functionality of the human brain's neural networks. They are composed of interconnected nodes, called neurons, organized into layers, and capable of learning complex patterns from data. In this comprehensive overview, we'll delve into the fundamental concepts of neural networks, including their architecture, activation functions, training process, and practical examples.

1. Neural Network Architecture:

Neural networks consist of three main types of layers:

- **Input Layer:** This layer receives the raw input data, such as images, text, or numerical features.
- **Hidden Layers:** Intermediate layers between the input and output layers. They perform computations on the input data through weighted connections and apply activation functions to introduce non-linearity.

- **Output Layer:** The final layer of the neural network, responsible for producing the model's predictions or outputs.

2. Activation Functions:

Activation functions introduce non-linearity into neural networks, allowing them to model complex relationships in data. Common activation functions include:

- **Sigmoid:** Maps input values to the range [0, 1], suitable for binary classification tasks.
- **ReLU (Rectified Linear Unit):** Returns the input if it is positive, otherwise returns zero, addressing the vanishing gradient problem and accelerating convergence in training.
- **Tanh (Hyperbolic Tangent):** Similar to the sigmoid function but maps input values to the range [-1, 1].

3. Training Process:

The training process of neural networks involves the following key steps:

- **Forward Propagation:** During forward propagation, input data is passed through the network, and computations are performed layer by layer to generate predictions.
- **Loss Calculation:** The loss function measures the discrepancy between the predicted outputs and the actual target values.
- **Backpropagation:** Backpropagation is a crucial step in training neural networks. It computes the gradients of the loss function with respect to the model parameters using the chain rule of calculus.
- **Parameter Updates:** Optimization algorithms, such as stochastic gradient descent (SGD) or Adam, are used to update the model parameters based on the computed gradients to minimize the loss function.

4. Practical Examples:

Let's consider a practical example of using a neural network for image classification:

```python
import tensorflow as tf
from tensorflow.keras import layers, models
# Define the neural network architecture
model = models.Sequential([
layers.Conv2D(32, (3, 3), activation='relu', input_shape=(28, 28, 1)),
layers.MaxPooling2D((2, 2)),
layers.Conv2D(64, (3, 3), activation='relu'),
layers.MaxPooling2D((2, 2)),
layers.Conv2D(64, (3, 3), activation='relu'),
layers.Flatten(),
layers.Dense(64, activation='relu'),
layers.Dense(10, activation='softmax')
])
# Compile the model
model.compile(optimizer='adam',
loss='sparse_categorical_crossentropy',
metrics=['accuracy'])
# Train the model
model.fit(train_images, train_labels, epochs=10, valida-
tion_data=(test_images, test_labels))
```

In this example, we define a convolutional neural network (CNN) architecture using the Keras API with TensorFlow backend for image classification tasks on the MNIST dataset.

Neural networks serve as the backbone of deep learning, enabling computers to learn complex patterns and make predictions from data. Understanding the architecture, activation functions, training process, and practical examples of neural networks is essential for building and deploying effective deep learning models across various domains, including computer vision, natural language processing, and health-care. Continued exploration and experimentation with neural network architectures and techniques are crucial for advancing the field of deep learning and solving real-world challenges.

Building Blocks of Deep Learning:

Deep learning encompasses a range of techniques and methodologies for training artificial neural networks to learn from data. Understanding the fundamental building blocks of deep learning is essential for effectively designing, training, and deploying neural network models. In this comprehensive overview, we'll delve into the key components and building blocks of deep learning, including neural network layers, activation functions, loss functions, optimization algorithms, and regularization techniques, with practical examples to illustrate their usage and functionality.

1. **Neural Network Layers:**

Neural network layers are the basic building blocks responsible for processing and transforming input data. Common types of layers include:

- **Dense (Fully Connected) Layer:** Each neuron in the layer is connected to every neuron in the preceding layer, performing a weighted sum of inputs followed by an activation function.
- **Convolutional Layer:** Applies convolution operations to the input data, extracting spatial features through filters or kernels.
- **Pooling Layer:** Reduces the spatial dimensions of the input data, helping to reduce computational complexity and prevent overfitting.
- **Recurrent Layer:** Processes sequential data by maintaining state information across time steps, commonly used in tasks like natural language processing and time series analysis.

2. Activation Functions:

Activation functions introduce non-linearity into neural networks, allowing them to model complex relationships in data. Popular activation functions include:

- **ReLU (Rectified Linear Unit):** Returns the input if it is positive, otherwise returns zero, addressing the vanishing gradient problem and accelerating convergence in training.
- **Sigmoid:** Maps input values to the range [0, 1], suitable for binary classification tasks.
- **Tanh (Hyperbolic Tangent):** Similar to the sigmoid function but maps input values to the range [-1, 1].

3. Loss Functions:

Loss functions quantify the discrepancy between the predicted outputs of a neural network model and the actual target values. The choice of loss function depends on the nature of the problem, such as classification or regression tasks. Common loss functions include:

- **Mean Squared Error (MSE):** Suitable for regression tasks, computes the average squared difference between predicted and actual values.
- **Binary Cross-Entropy Loss:** Used for binary classification tasks, measures the difference between predicted probabilities and true binary labels.
- **Categorical Cross-Entropy Loss:** Applied to multi-class classification tasks, measures the difference between predicted class probabilities and true class labels.

4. Optimization Algorithms:

Optimization algorithms adjust the parameters of a neural network during training to minimize the loss function. Popular optimization algorithms include:

- **Stochastic Gradient Descent (SGD):** Updates model parameters based on the gradient of the loss function with respect to each parameter.
- **Adam:** An adaptive optimization algorithm that combines ideas from RMSProp and Momentum, providing fast convergence and robustness to hyperparameters.

5. Regularization Techniques:

Regularization techniques prevent overfitting by imposing constraints on the complexity of the model. Common regularization techniques include:

- **L1 and L2 Regularization:** Add penalties to the loss function based on the magnitudes of the model parameters to discourage large parameter values.
- **Dropout:** Randomly sets a fraction of input units to zero during training, preventing units from co-adapting and acting as "regularization by noise."

Practical Examples:

Let's consider an example of building a convolutional neural network (CNN) for image classification using the Keras API with TensorFlow backend:

```python
import tensorflow as tf
from tensorflow.keras import layers, models
# Define the CNN architecture
model = models.Sequential([
layers.Conv2D(32, (3, 3), activation='relu', input_shape=(28, 28, 1)),
layers.MaxPooling2D((2, 2)),
layers.Conv2D(64, (3, 3), activation='relu'),
layers.MaxPooling2D((2, 2)),
layers.Conv2D(64, (3, 3), activation='relu'),
layers.Flatten(),
```

```
layers.Dense(64, activation='relu'),
layers.Dense(10, activation='softmax')
])
# Compile the model
model.compile(optimizer='adam',
loss='sparse_categorical_crossentropy',
metrics=['accuracy'])
# Train the model
model.fit(train_images, train_labels, epochs=10, valida-
tion_data=(test_images, test_labels))
```

In this example, we define a CNN architecture for image classification tasks on the MNIST dataset using convolutional and dense layers, with ReLU activation functions and the Adam optimizer.

Understanding the building blocks of deep learning is essential for effectively designing, training, and deploying neural network models across various domains. By mastering the concepts of neural network layers, activation functions, loss functions, optimization algorithms, and regularization techniques, practitioners can develop robust and scalable deep learning models capable of solving complex real-world problems. Continuously exploring advanced techniques and experimenting with different architectures are crucial for pushing the boundaries of deep learning and driving innovation in the field.

Convolutional Neural Networks (CNNs):

Convolutional Neural Networks (CNNs) are a specialized type of neural network designed for processing structured grid-like data, such as images and time series. CNNs have revolutionized various fields, particularly computer vision, by enabling tasks such as image classification, object detection, and image segmentation. In this comprehensive overview, we'll explore the fundamental concepts of CNNs, including their architecture, operations, common layers, and practical examples to illustrate their usage and effectiveness.

1. Architecture of Convolutional Neural Networks:

CNNs consist of a series of interconnected layers, each performing specific operations on the input data. The typical architecture of a CNN includes the following components:

- **Convolutional Layers:** These layers apply convolution operations to the input data, extracting spatial features through learned filters or kernels.
- **Activation Functions:** Activation functions introduce non-linearity into the network, allowing it to model complex relationships in the data. Common choices include ReLU, sigmoid, and tanh.
- **Pooling Layers:** Pooling layers reduce the spatial dimensions of the feature maps, helping to extract dominant features and reduce computational complexity.
- **Fully Connected Layers:** Also known as dense layers, these layers connect every neuron in one layer to every neuron in the next layer, performing classification or regression tasks.

2. Operations in Convolutional Neural Networks:

- **Convolution:** Convolution involves applying a filter to the input data to produce a feature map, capturing spatial patterns such as edges, textures, and shapes.
- **Activation:** After convolution, an activation function is applied element-wise to the feature map, introducing non-linearity and enabling the network to learn complex patterns.
- **Pooling:** Pooling operations (e.g., max pooling, average pooling) downsample the feature maps, reducing their spatial dimensions while preserving important features.

- **Fully Connected Layers:** The output of the convolutional and pooling layers is flattened and fed into one or more fully connected layers, which perform classification or regression tasks.

3. Common Convolutional Neural Network Layers:

- **Conv2D Layer:** Applies 2D convolutional operations to the input data, extracting spatial features through learned filters.
- **MaxPooling2D Layer:** Performs max pooling operations to downsample the spatial dimensions of the feature maps.
- **Flatten Layer:** Flattens the output of the convolutional and pooling layers into a one-dimensional vector, ready for input into the fully connected layers.
- **Dense Layer:** Also known as fully connected layers, these layers connect every neuron in one layer to every neuron in the next layer, performing classification or regression tasks.

4. Practical Examples:

Let's consider an example of building a CNN for image classification using the Keras API with TensorFlow backend:

```python
import tensorflow as tf
from tensorflow.keras import layers, models
# Define the CNN architecture
model = models.Sequential([
layers.Conv2D(32, (3, 3), activation='relu', input_shape=(28, 28, 1)),
layers.MaxPooling2D((2, 2)),
layers.Conv2D(64, (3, 3), activation='relu'),
layers.MaxPooling2D((2, 2)),
layers.Conv2D(64, (3, 3), activation='relu'),
layers.Flatten(),
layers.Dense(64, activation='relu'),
layers.Dense(10, activation='softmax')
])
```

```python
# Compile the model
model.compile(optimizer='adam',
loss='sparse_categorical_crossentropy',
metrics=['accuracy'])
# Train the model
model.fit(train_images, train_labels, epochs=10, validation_data=(test_images, test_labels))
```

In this example, we define a CNN architecture for image classification tasks on the MNIST dataset using convolutional and dense layers, with ReLU activation functions and the Adam optimizer.

Convolutional Neural Networks (CNNs) are powerful deep learning models designed for processing structured grid-like data, particularly images. By leveraging operations such as convolution, activation, pooling, and fully connected layers, CNNs can automatically learn hierarchical representations of data, enabling tasks such as image classification, object detection, and image segmentation. Understanding the architecture, operations, and common layers of CNNs is essential for effectively designing, training, and deploying neural network models in various domains, from computer vision to healthcare and beyond. Continued exploration and experimentation with CNN architectures and techniques are crucial for pushing the boundaries of deep learning and advancing the state-of-the-art in artificial intelligence.

Recurrent Neural Networks (RNNs):

Recurrent Neural Networks (RNNs) are a class of neural networks designed to model sequential data by capturing temporal dependencies and relationships between elements in a sequence. RNNs have widespread applications in natural language processing, speech recognition, time series analysis, and more. In this comprehensive overview, we'll explore the fundamental concepts of RNNs, including their architecture, operations, training process, and practical examples to illustrate their usage and effectiveness.

1. **Architecture of Recurrent Neural Networks:**

Unlike feedforward neural networks, which process input data in a single pass, RNNs have loops within their architecture, allowing them to maintain internal state and process sequences of data. The typical architecture of an RNN includes the following components:

- **Recurrent Connections:** Recurrent connections enable information to persist across time steps in the sequence, allowing RNNs to capture temporal dependencies.
- **Hidden State (or Memory):** At each time step, the RNN maintains a hidden state that encodes information about the sequence seen so far.
- **Input and Output Layers:** Similar to feedforward neural networks, RNNs have input and output layers that interact with the external environment and produce predictions.

2. **Operations in Recurrent Neural Networks:**

- **Forward Pass:** During the forward pass, RNNs process input sequences one time step at a time, updating the hidden state based on both the current input and the previous hidden state.
- **Backward Pass:** In the backward pass, gradients are propagated through time using techniques like backpropagation through time (BPTT), enabling the RNN to learn from sequential data.

3. **Types of Recurrent Neural Networks:**

- **Vanilla RNN:** The basic form of RNN, where the hidden state at each time step is computed using a simple linear transformation and a non-linear activation function.

- **Long Short-Term Memory (LSTM):** An advanced variant of RNN designed to address the vanishing gradient problem and capture long-range dependencies more effectively.
- **Gated Recurrent Unit (GRU):** A simplified version of LSTM with fewer parameters, making it computationally more efficient while still addressing the vanishing gradient problem.

4. Practical Examples:

Let's consider an example of using an LSTM-based RNN for sentiment analysis on movie reviews:

```
import tensorflow as tf
from tensorflow.keras import layers, models
# Define the LSTM-based RNN architecture
model = models.Sequential([
layers.Embedding(vocab_size, embedding_dim, input_length=max_length),
layers.LSTM(64, return_sequences=True),
layers.LSTM(64),
layers.Dense(64, activation='relu'),
layers.Dense(1, activation='sigmoid')
])
# Compile the model
model.compile(optimizer='adam',
loss='binary_crossentropy',
metrics=['accuracy'])
# Train the model
model.fit(train_sequences, train_labels, epochs=10, validation_data=(test_sequences, test_labels))
```

In this example, we define an LSTM-based RNN architecture for sentiment analysis tasks on movie reviews. The model takes sequences of word embeddings as input and produces binary sentiment predictions.

Recurrent Neural Networks (RNNs) are powerful deep learning models capable of processing sequential data and capturing temporal dependencies. By leveraging recurrent connections and hidden states, RNNs can model complex sequences of data and perform tasks such as sequence prediction, language modeling, and time series forecasting. Understanding the architecture, operations, and types of RNNs is essential for effectively designing, training, and deploying neural network models in various domains. Continued exploration and experimentation with RNN architectures and techniques are crucial for advancing the state-of-the-art in deep learning and addressing real-world challenges in sequential data analysis.

Conclusion:

Deep learning basics encompass the foundational concepts necessary for understanding and building neural network models. By grasping the principles of neural networks, activation functions, loss functions, optimization algorithms, and regularization techniques, practitioners can effectively design, train, and deploy deep learning models for a wide range of tasks, from image recognition to natural language processing and beyond. Continuously exploring advanced topics and staying updated with the latest developments in the field are essential for mastering deep learning techniques and tackling increasingly complex problems.

Chapter 8: Advanced Topics in Machine Learning

Machine learning is a rapidly evolving field with various advanced topics that delve into sophisticated techniques, algorithms, and methodologies to address complex problems and extract deeper insights from data. In this comprehensive overview, we'll explore some of the advanced topics in machine learning, including ensemble learning, transfer learning, generative adversarial networks (GANs), reinforcement learning, and Bayesian methods, with practical examples to illustrate their applications and effectiveness.

1. Ensemble Learning:

Ensemble learning involves combining multiple machine learning models to improve predictive performance and generalization. Common ensemble methods include:

Random Forest:

A collection of decision trees trained on different subsets of the data, with predictions aggregated through voting or averaging.

Ensemble learning is a powerful technique in machine learning that involves combining multiple models to improve predictive performance and robustness. Random Forest is a popular ensemble learning algorithm that builds multiple decision trees during training and combines their predictions through voting or averaging. In this comprehensive overview, we'll delve into the workings of Random Forest, its advantages, implementation details, and provide practical examples to illustrate its effectiveness.

1. How Random Forest Works:

- **Decision Trees:** Random Forest consists of a collection of decision trees, where each tree is trained independently on a random subset of the training data.
- **Random Feature Selection:** At each split in the decision tree, a random subset of features is considered for splitting, reducing the correlation between individual trees.
- **Bootstrap Aggregation (Bagging):** Random Forest employs bootstrap sampling to create multiple subsets of the training data, ensuring diversity among the trees.
- **Voting or Averaging:** During prediction, the ensemble of decision trees combines their individual predictions through voting (for classification tasks) or averaging (for regression tasks) to produce the final output.

2. Advantages of Random Forest:

- **Robust to Overfitting:** Random Forest mitigates overfitting by combining multiple weak learners (decision trees) trained on different subsets of data.
- **Handles High-Dimensional Data:** Random Forest performs well with high-dimensional data and can handle datasets with a large number of features.
- **Efficient Parallelization:** Training and prediction in Random Forest can be easily parallelized, making it suitable for large-scale datasets and distributed computing environments.

3. Implementation of Random Forest:

Python's scikit-learn library provides an easy-to-use implementation of Random Forest. Here's how to train and use a Random Forest classifier:

```
from sklearn.ensemble import RandomForestClassifier
# Initialize Random Forest classifier
rf_classifier = RandomForestClassifier(n_estimators=100, max_depth=10, random_state=42)
# Train the classifier
rf_classifier.fit(X_train, y_train)
# Make predictions
y_pred = rf_classifier.predict(X_test)
```

4. Practical Examples:

- **Credit Risk Assessment:** In banking and finance, Random Forest can be used to assess the credit risk of loan applicants by combining the predictions of multiple decision trees trained on historical data.

- **Medical Diagnosis:** Random Forest can assist in medical diagnosis tasks by analyzing patient data (e.g., symptoms, medical history) to predict the likelihood of certain diseases, leveraging the ensemble of decision trees for accurate predictions.

- **Customer Churn Prediction:** In customer relationship management, Random Forest can predict customer churn (i.e., the likelihood of customers leaving) by analyzing customer behavior and demographics, helping businesses proactively retain customers.

Random Forest is a versatile and powerful ensemble learning algorithm that excels in various machine learning tasks, including classification and regression. By leveraging the collective wisdom of multiple decision trees trained on diverse subsets of data, Random Forest delivers robust predictions while mitigating overfitting. Its ease of use, scalability, and efficiency make it a popular choice for both beginners and experienced practitioners in the field of machine learning. With its numerous applications across industries, Random Forest continues to be a valuable tool for solving real-world problems and extracting actionable insights from data.

Gradient Boosting Machines (GBM):

Sequentially builds a collection of weak learners (typically decision trees), with each subsequent learner correcting the errors of the previous ones.

Gradient Boosting Machines (GBM) are powerful ensemble learning algorithms that combine multiple weak learners (typically decision trees) sequentially to improve predictive performance. GBM iteratively trains new models to correct the errors of the previous ones, gradually optimizing the overall prediction. In this comprehensive overview, we'll delve into the workings of Gradient Boosting Machines, their advantages, implementation details, and provide practical examples to illustrate their effectiveness.

1. How Gradient Boosting Machines Work:

- **Weak Learners:** GBM builds an ensemble of weak learners, usually decision trees, where each tree is trained on the residuals (errors) of the previous model.
- **Gradient Descent:** GBM minimizes a predefined loss function (e.g., mean squared error for regression, cross-entropy loss for classification) by iteratively updating the model parameters in the direction that reduces the loss gradient.
- **Sequential Training:** In each iteration, GBM trains a new weak learner to predict the residuals of the previous model, effectively reducing the error of the ensemble.
- **Combining Predictions:** The final prediction is obtained by summing the predictions of all weak learners in the ensemble.

2. Advantages of Gradient Boosting Machines:

- **High Predictive Accuracy:** GBM often achieves state-of-the-art performance on various machine learning tasks, including regression and classification, by iteratively refining predictions.
- **Handles Heterogeneous Data:** GBM can handle heterogeneous data types and feature spaces, including numerical, categorical, and text data.
- **Feature Importance:** GBM provides insights into feature importance, allowing users to identify the most influential variables in the predictive model.

3. Implementation of Gradient Boosting Machines:

Python's scikit-learn library provides an efficient implementation of Gradient Boosting Machines. Here's how to train and use a Gradient Boosting classifier:

```
from sklearn.ensemble import GradientBoostingClassifier
# Initialize Gradient Boosting classifier
gb_classifier = GradientBoostingClassifier(n_estimators=100, learning_rate=0.1, max_depth=3, random_state=42)
# Train the classifier
gb_classifier.fit(X_train, y_train)
# Make predictions
y_pred = gb_classifier.predict(X_test)
```

4. Practical Examples:

- **Click-Through Rate Prediction:** In online advertising, GBM can predict the probability of a user clicking on an ad based on features such as user demographics, ad content, and browsing history, enabling targeted ad placement.
- **Customer Churn Prediction:** In customer relationship management, GBM can predict the likelihood of customers leaving a subscription service or canceling a subscription based on

historical data, helping businesses retain customers through proactive retention strategies.

- **Stock Price Prediction:** In finance, GBM can forecast stock prices by analyzing historical market data, fundamental indicators, and sentiment analysis from news articles, enabling investors to make informed decisions.

Gradient Boosting Machines (GBM) are powerful ensemble learning algorithms that excel in various machine learning tasks, including classification, regression, and ranking. By iteratively training weak learners to correct the errors of the ensemble, GBM produces accurate predictions and provides insights into feature importance. Its ease of use, scalability, and robustness make it a popular choice for both beginners and experienced practitioners in the field of machine learning. With its numerous applications across industries, Gradient Boosting Machines continue to be a valuable tool for solving real-world problems and driving business insights from data.

AdaBoost:

Trains a sequence of weak learners, assigning higher weights to misclassified samples at each iteration to focus on difficult-to-classify instances.

Example: Using ensemble learning for classification tasks such as customer churn prediction or fraud detection, where multiple models are combined to achieve higher accuracy and robustness.

2. Transfer Learning:

Transfer learning involves leveraging knowledge gained from one task to improve performance on another related task. Instead of training a model from scratch, transfer learning allows models to transfer learned representations or features from a pre-trained model to a new task.

Example: Fine-tuning a pre-trained convolutional neural network (CNN) on a new dataset for image classification tasks. The pre-trained CNN, such as VGG16 or ResNet, has learned generic features from a large dataset like ImageNet, which can be adapted and fine-tuned for specific classification tasks with limited data.

3. Generative Adversarial Networks (GANs):

GANs are a class of deep learning models that consist of two neural networks, a generator and a discriminator, trained in an adversarial manner. The generator learns to generate realistic data samples (e.g., images, text) from random noise, while the discriminator learns to distinguish between real and fake samples.

Example: Generating realistic images of human faces using a GAN architecture such as Deep Convolutional GAN (DCGAN) or Progressive GAN (PGAN). GANs have applications in image generation, style transfer, and data augmentation.

4. Reinforcement Learning:

Reinforcement learning (RL) is a type of machine learning where agents learn to make sequential decisions by interacting with an environment to maximize cumulative rewards. RL algorithms learn through trial and error, optimizing policies to achieve long-term goals.

Example: Training an RL agent to play Atari games or board games like Go or chess. The agent learns optimal strategies by receiving feedback (rewards) from the environment based on its actions, gradually improving its performance over time.

5. Bayesian Methods:

Bayesian methods in machine learning involve probabilistic modeling and inference, allowing for uncertainty quantification and principled decision-making under uncertainty. Bayesian approaches can incorporate prior knowledge, update beliefs based on new evidence, and provide probabilistic predictions.

Example: Bayesian optimization for hyperparameter tuning in machine learning models. By modeling the objective function as a Gaussian process, Bayesian optimization efficiently searches the hyperparameter space to find the optimal configuration while considering uncertainty.

Conclusion:

Advanced topics in machine learning encompass a wide range of techniques and methodologies that enable practitioners to tackle complex problems and extract deeper insights from data. By leveraging ensemble learning, transfer learning, generative adversarial networks (GANs), reinforcement learning, Bayesian methods, and other advanced techniques, machine learning practitioners can push the boundaries of what's possible and address real-world challenges in various domains, from computer vision and natural language processing to robotics and healthcare. Continued exploration and experimentation with advanced topics are essential for staying at the forefront of machine learning research and innovation.

Ensemble Learning Techniques:

Ensemble learning is a powerful technique in machine learning where multiple models are combined to improve overall performance. By aggregating the predictions of diverse models, ensemble methods can reduce overfitting, increase predictive accuracy, and provide robustness to noisy data. In this comprehensive overview, we'll explore ensemble learning techniques, including bagging, boosting, stacking, and their practical applications across various domains.

1. **Bagging (Bootstrap Aggregating):**

   Bagging is an ensemble learning technique that involves training multiple base learners independently on different subsets of the training data. Each base learner has equal weight in the final prediction, and the ensemble combines their predictions through averaging (for regression) or voting (for classification).

   Example: Random Forest is a popular bagging algorithm that combines multiple decision trees trained on bootstrap samples of the training data. It is widely used for tasks such as classification, regression, and anomaly detection.

2. **Boosting:**

Boosting is an ensemble learning technique that focuses on training a sequence of weak learners sequentially, with each subsequent model correcting the errors of the previous ones. The final prediction is obtained by combining the predictions of all weak learners, typically using a weighted sum.

Example: Gradient Boosting Machines (GBM) and AdaBoost are popular boosting algorithms. GBM iteratively fits new models to the residuals of the previous models, optimizing a predefined loss function. AdaBoost assigns higher weights to misclassified samples at each iteration, focusing on difficult-to-classify instances.

3. **Stacking:**

Stacking, also known as stacked generalization, involves training multiple base learners and then using a meta-learner to combine their predictions. Instead of simple averaging or voting, stacking learns how to best combine the predictions of the base learners using a higher-level model.

Example: In a stacking ensemble, diverse base models such as decision trees, support vector machines, and neural networks are trained on the training data. The meta-learner, often a linear regression or neural network, learns to combine the predictions of the base models to produce the final output.

4. **Practical Applications of Ensemble Learning:**

- **Credit Risk Assessment:** Ensemble learning techniques can be applied to predict credit risk by combining the predictions of multiple models trained on different features or subsets of data, helping financial institutions make more informed lending decisions.

- **Medical Diagnosis:** Ensemble learning can aid in medical diagnosis by aggregating the predictions of diverse models trained on patient data (e.g., symptoms, medical history). The ensemble can provide more reliable diagnoses and assist healthcare professionals in treatment planning.

- **Predictive Maintenance:** In manufacturing, ensemble learning can predict equipment failures by combining the outputs of various machine learning models trained on sensor data, maintenance logs, and historical failure records. Early detection of potential failures helps minimize downtime and maintenance costs.

Ensemble learning techniques are powerful tools in the machine learning toolbox, capable of improving predictive accuracy, reducing overfitting, and providing robustness to noisy data. By combining the strengths of multiple models, ensemble methods can tackle complex real-world problems across various domains, from finance and healthcare to manufacturing and beyond. Understanding and leveraging ensemble learning techniques are essential skills for machine learning practitioners aiming to build high-performing predictive models and extract actionable insights from data.

Reinforcement Learning:

Reinforcement Learning (RL) is a powerful paradigm in machine learning that enables agents to learn how to make sequential decisions by interacting with an environment. Through trial and error, the agent learns to take actions that maximize cumulative rewards, achieving long-term goals. In this comprehensive overview, we'll explore the principles of Reinforcement Learning, its key components, algorithms, and practical examples across various domains.

1. **Principles of Reinforcement Learning:**

- **Agent:** The learner or decision-maker that interacts with the environment.

- **Environment:** The external system with which the agent interacts and receives feedback.
- **State:** The current situation or configuration of the environment.
- **Action:** The decision made by the agent to transition from one state to another.
- **Reward:** Feedback from the environment indicating the desirability of the action taken by the agent.
- **Policy:** The strategy or rule that the agent follows to select actions in different states.

2. Components of Reinforcement Learning:

- **Value Function:** Estimates the long-term cumulative reward that an agent can expect to receive from a given state or action.
- **Q-Function (Action-Value Function):** Estimates the expected cumulative reward of taking a specific action in a given state.
- **Policy Gradient:** Directly learns the policy function, mapping states to actions, by optimizing the expected cumulative reward through gradient descent.

3. Reinforcement Learning Algorithms:

- **Q-Learning:** An off-policy RL algorithm that learns the Q-function iteratively through temporal difference updates, enabling the agent to find an optimal policy.
- **Deep Q-Networks (DQN):** Combines Q-learning with deep neural networks to approximate the Q-function in high-dimensional state spaces, enabling RL in complex environments such as video games.
- **Policy Gradient Methods:** Directly optimize the policy function by computing gradients of expected rewards with respect to

policy parameters, enabling RL in continuous action spaces and stochastic environments.

4. Practical Examples of Reinforcement Learning:

- **Game Playing:** RL algorithms have achieved remarkable success in mastering complex games such as Chess, Go, and video games like Atari games. For example, AlphaGo, developed by DeepMind, uses RL to defeat human world champions in the game of Go.
- **Robotics:** RL enables robots to learn complex motor skills and manipulate objects in unstructured environments. RL algorithms can train robotic agents to perform tasks such as grasping objects, navigating obstacles, and even assisting in household chores.
- **Autonomous Vehicles:** RL plays a crucial role in training autonomous vehicles to make decisions in dynamic and uncertain environments. RL algorithms can optimize driving policies to navigate safely, efficiently, and adaptively in real-world traffic scenarios.

Reinforcement Learning is a versatile and powerful paradigm in machine learning that enables agents to learn how to make sequential decisions through trial and error. By interacting with an environment and receiving feedback in the form of rewards, RL algorithms can learn complex behaviors and achieve long-term goals in diverse domains. Understanding the principles, components, and algorithms of Reinforcement Learning is essential for building intelligent systems capable of autonomous decision-making and adaptation to dynamic environments. Continued research and development in RL hold the promise of revolutionizing fields such as robotics, autonomous systems, and personalized assistance.

Natural Language Processing (NLP):

Natural Language Processing (NLP) is a subfield of artificial intelligence that focuses on the interaction between computers and human languages. It enables machines to understand, interpret, and generate human language in a meaningful way. In this comprehensive overview, we'll explore the principles of Natural Language Processing, its key components, techniques, and practical examples across various applications.

1. Principles of Natural Language Processing:

- **Tokenization:** The process of breaking text into smaller units, such as words or subwords, called tokens.
- **Text Normalization:** Converting text to a standard form, including tasks like lowercasing, stemming, and lemmatization.
- **Named Entity Recognition (NER):** Identifying and classifying named entities such as people, organizations, locations, and dates in text.
- **Part-of-Speech (POS) Tagging:** Assigning grammatical categories (e.g., noun, verb, adjective) to words in a sentence.

2. Key Components of Natural Language Processing:

- **Text Representation:** Methods for representing text data in a numerical format suitable for machine learning models, such as Bag-of-Words (BoW), Term Frequency-Inverse Document Frequency (TF-IDF), and word embeddings like Word2Vec and GloVe.
- **Language Models:** Statistical models that predict the next word in a sequence of text, trained on large corpora of text data. Examples include n-gram models, recurrent neural networks (RNNs), and transformer models like BERT and GPT.

- **Semantic Analysis:** Techniques for understanding the meaning of text, including sentiment analysis, topic modeling, and semantic similarity.
- **Sequence-to-Sequence Models:** Neural network architectures that translate one sequence of text into another, commonly used for tasks like machine translation, text summarization, and question answering.

3. Techniques in Natural Language Processing:

- **Sentiment Analysis:** Determining the sentiment or emotion expressed in a piece of text, such as positive, negative, or neutral. Sentiment analysis has applications in social media monitoring, customer feedback analysis, and brand reputation management.
- **Machine Translation:** Automatically translating text from one language to another, enabling cross-lingual communication and content localization. Example systems include Google Translate, DeepL, and Microsoft Translator.
- **Named Entity Recognition (NER):** Identifying and categorizing entities mentioned in text, such as people, organizations, locations, and dates. NER is essential for tasks like information extraction, entity linking, and question answering systems.
- **Text Generation:** Generating human-like text based on input prompts or contexts, often using generative models like recurrent neural networks (RNNs), transformer models, and language models like GPT and BERT.

4. Practical Examples of Natural Language Processing:

- **Chatbots:** NLP-powered chatbots interact with users in natural language, answering questions, providing information, and assisting with tasks. Examples include customer service chatbots, virtual assistants like Siri and Alexa, and conversational agents for education and entertainment.

- **Document Summarization:** NLP algorithms can automatically summarize large documents or articles, extracting key information and condensing it into shorter summaries. Summarization techniques include extractive summarization (e.g., selecting important sentences) and abstractive summarization (e.g., generating summaries using natural language generation).

- **Information Extraction:** NLP systems can extract structured information from unstructured text, such as extracting named entities, relations between entities, and events mentioned in news articles or research papers. Information extraction has applications in knowledge graph construction, database population, and information retrieval.

Natural Language Processing (NLP) is a fundamental area of study in artificial intelligence that enables machines to understand and process human language. By leveraging techniques such as text representation, language models, semantic analysis, and machine learning algorithms, NLP systems can perform a wide range of tasks, including sentiment analysis, machine translation, named entity recognition, and text generation. Practical applications of NLP span across industries, including healthcare, finance, e-commerce, education, and entertainment, revolutionizing how we interact with and extract insights from textual data. Continued advancements in NLP hold the promise of further enhancing human-machine communication and enabling intelligent systems capable of understanding and generating natural language with increasing accuracy and sophistication.

Time Series Analysis:

Time Series Analysis is a specialized field of machine learning and statistics focused on understanding and forecasting data points collected over time. It encompasses techniques to extract meaningful insights, detect patterns, and make predictions from time-ordered data. In this comprehensive overview, we'll explore the principles of Time Series Analysis, its key components, methods, and practical examples across various domains.

1. **Principles of Time Series Analysis:**

- **Time Series Data:** Data collected at regular intervals over time, such as stock prices, weather observations, sensor readings, and economic indicators.
- **Trend:** The long-term movement or directionality in the data, indicating whether values are increasing, decreasing, or remaining constant over time.
- **Seasonality:** Patterns that repeat at fixed intervals within the data, often associated with seasonal variations, holidays, or periodic events.
- **Stationarity:** A property of time series data where statistical properties such as mean, variance, and autocorrelation remain constant over time. Stationarity simplifies modeling and forecasting.

2. **Key Components of Time Series Analysis:**

- **Exploratory Data Analysis (EDA):** Visualizing and analyzing time series data to identify trends, seasonality, outliers, and other patterns using techniques like line plots, histograms, auto-correlation plots, and decomposition.
- **Time Series Decomposition:** Separating a time series into its constituent components, including trend, seasonality, and noise, using methods like additive decomposition or multiplicative decomposition.

- **Forecasting:** Predicting future values of a time series based on historical observations using statistical models, machine learning algorithms, or hybrid approaches.

3. Methods in Time Series Analysis:

- **Autoregressive Integrated Moving Average (ARIMA):** A popular linear model for time series forecasting that combines autoregression (AR), differencing (I), and moving average (MA) components to capture temporal dependencies and trends.
- **Seasonal ARIMA (SARIMA):** An extension of ARIMA that incorporates seasonal components to model and forecast time series data with seasonal patterns.
- **Exponential Smoothing Methods:** Techniques that assign exponentially decreasing weights to past observations, such as Simple Exponential Smoothing (SES), Double Exponential Smoothing (Holt's method), and Triple Exponential Smoothing (Holt-Winters method).
- **Machine Learning Models:** Supervised learning algorithms like Support Vector Machines (SVM), Random Forests, Gradient Boosting Machines (GBM), and Long Short-Term Memory (LSTM) networks can be adapted for time series forecasting by treating the problem as a regression or classification task.

4. Practical Examples of Time Series Analysis:

- **Stock Market Prediction:** Time series analysis is widely used in finance to predict stock prices, identify trends, and inform investment decisions. Techniques like ARIMA, LSTM networks, and hybrid models are employed to forecast stock prices and volatility.
- **Demand Forecasting:** Retailers use time series analysis to forecast product demand, optimize inventory management, and plan

production schedules. Accurate demand forecasting helps minimize stockouts, reduce inventory costs, and improve customer satisfaction.

- **Energy Consumption Forecasting:** Utilities and energy companies use time series analysis to predict energy demand, optimize energy production and distribution, and plan maintenance schedules for power grids and infrastructure.
- **Traffic and Transportation Planning:** Time series analysis is applied in traffic management systems to predict traffic congestion, optimize traffic flow, and plan infrastructure development and transportation services.

Time Series Analysis is a critical area of study in machine learning and statistics, enabling the analysis, modeling, and forecasting of time-ordered data across various domains. By understanding and leveraging temporal patterns, trends, and dependencies within time series data, practitioners can extract valuable insights, make informed decisions, and predict future outcomes. From finance and retail to energy and transportation, time series analysis plays a vital role in optimizing operations, improving resource allocation, and enhancing decision-making processes. Continued advancements in time series analysis methodologies and techniques hold the promise of further enhancing predictive accuracy, scalability, and interpretability, driving innovation and addressing complex challenges in diverse industries.

Chapter 9: Model Evaluation and Hyperparameter Tuning

Model evaluation and hyperparameter tuning are crucial steps in the machine learning pipeline that involve assessing the performance of models and optimizing their hyperparameters to improve predictive accuracy and generalization. In this comprehensive overview, we'll explore the principles of model evaluation, hyperparameter tuning techniques, and practical examples to illustrate their importance and impact on model performance.

1. **Model Evaluation:**

Model evaluation is the process of assessing the performance of machine learning models using various metrics and techniques. The goal is to understand how well a model generalizes to unseen data and whether it meets the requirements of the problem at hand.

Key Concepts:

Train-Validation-Test Split:

Data is divided into three sets: training data for model training, validation data for hyperparameter tuning, and test data for final evaluation. This ensures unbiased assessment of model performance.

1. Key Concepts: Train-Validation-Test Split

The Train-Validation-Test split is a fundamental concept in machine learning that ensures unbiased evaluation of model performance and generalization to unseen data. It involves partitioning the dataset into three subsets: the training set, validation set, and test set.

Explanation:

- **Training Set:** This subset of the data is used to train the machine learning model. The model learns patterns and relationships in the data to make predictions. The training set typically constitutes the largest portion of the dataset.
- **Validation Set:** The validation set is used to evaluate the performance of the model during training and hyperparameter tuning. It helps to assess how well the model generalizes to unseen data and allows for comparison of different models or hyperparameter configurations.
- **Test Set:** The test set serves as a final evaluation of the model's performance after training and hyperparameter tuning. It provides an unbiased estimate of the model's ability to generalize to new, unseen data. The test set should only be used once, after all model development and tuning steps are complete.

Example:

Consider a dataset containing historical housing prices and features such as square footage, number of bedrooms, and location. The goal is to build a machine learning model to predict the price of houses.

- **Step 1: Train-Validation-Test Split:**
  - The dataset is divided into three subsets: training set, validation set, and test set.
  - For example, 70% of the data may be allocated to the training set, 15% to the validation set, and 15% to the test set.

- **Step 2: Training the Model:**
  - The machine learning model is trained on the training set using various algorithms and techniques.
  - For instance, a regression model like Random Forest or Gradient Boosting is trained to learn the relationships between the features and the target variable (housing price).
- **Step 3: Validation for Hyperparameter Tuning:**
  - The model's performance is evaluated on the validation set to assess its predictive accuracy and identify areas for improvement.
  - Hyperparameters, such as the number of trees in a Random Forest or the learning rate in a Gradient Boosting model, are tuned using the validation set.
  - Different hyperparameter configurations are tested, and the one yielding the best performance on the validation set is selected.
- **Step 4: Final Evaluation on Test Set:**
  - Once the model and hyperparameters are finalized, the model's performance is evaluated on the test set.
  - The test set provides an unbiased estimate of the model's performance on unseen data, helping to gauge its real-world applicability.
  - Metrics such as mean squared error (MSE) or mean absolute error (MAE) are calculated to quantify the model's predictive accuracy.

Importance:

- **Unbiased Evaluation:** The Train-Validation-Test split ensures that the model's performance is evaluated on independent datasets, preventing overfitting and providing a reliable estimate of its generalization ability.

- **Hyperparameter Tuning:** The validation set is crucial for tuning model hyperparameters, such as regularization strength or learning rate, to optimize model performance without introducing bias.
- **Final Evaluation:** The test set serves as the ultimate benchmark for assessing the model's readiness for deployment in real-world applications, providing confidence in its performance on unseen data.

The Train-Validation-Test split is a fundamental concept in model evaluation that ensures the robustness and generalization of machine learning models. By partitioning the dataset into training, validation, and test sets, practitioners can develop and fine-tune models with confidence, leading to more accurate and reliable predictions in real-world scenarios.

Cross-Validation:

A technique for robust model evaluation by repeatedly splitting the data into training and validation sets. Common methods include k-fold cross-validation and stratified cross-validation.

Cross-validation is a robust technique used to evaluate the performance of machine learning models by systematically partitioning the dataset into multiple subsets and training the model on different combinations of these subsets. It helps to assess the model's generalization ability and reduce bias in performance estimation.

Explanation:

- **K-Fold Cross-Validation:** In k-fold cross-validation, the dataset is divided into k subsets of approximately equal size. The model is trained k times, each time using a different subset as the validation set and the remaining data as the training set. The performance metrics are averaged across the k folds to obtain an overall evaluation of the model.

- **Stratified Cross-Validation:** In stratified cross-validation, the class distribution of the target variable is preserved across each fold. This ensures that each fold represents a similar distribution of classes as the original dataset, reducing the risk of bias in model evaluation, especially for imbalanced datasets.
- **Leave-One-Out Cross-Validation (LOOCV):** LOOCV is a special case of k-fold cross-validation where k is equal to the number of samples in the dataset. In each iteration, one sample is held out as the validation set, and the model is trained on the remaining data. This process is repeated for each sample in the dataset, resulting in k iterations.

Example:

Consider a dataset containing patient data with features such as age, gender, and medical history, and the target variable indicating whether a patient has a certain medical condition. The goal is to build a machine learning model to predict the likelihood of a patient having the medical condition based on their features.

- **Step 1: K-Fold Cross-Validation:**
    - The dataset is divided into k folds, typically with k = 5 or 10.
    - For example, with k = 5, the dataset is split into five subsets of equal size.
- **Step 2: Model Training and Evaluation:**
    - The model is trained k times, each time using a different fold as the validation set and the remaining folds as the training set.
    - For each iteration, the model's performance metrics, such as accuracy, precision, recall, and F1 score, are computed on the validation set.
- **Step 3: Performance Aggregation:**

- ○ The performance metrics obtained from each fold are averaged to obtain a single estimate of the model's performance.
- ○ This aggregated performance metric serves as an unbiased evaluation of the model's generalization ability across different subsets of the data.

Importance:

- **Reduced Bias:** Cross-validation provides a more reliable estimate of a model's performance by averaging results across multiple iterations, reducing the risk of bias introduced by a single train-test split.
- **Optimal Hyperparameter Tuning:** Cross-validation is commonly used for hyperparameter tuning, allowing practitioners to assess the impact of hyperparameters on model performance across different subsets of the data.
- **Model Selection:** Cross-validation helps in comparing and selecting between different machine learning models or algorithms by evaluating their performance on multiple folds of the dataset.

Cross-validation is a powerful technique for model evaluation that helps to assess a machine learning model's performance across different subsets of the data, providing a more reliable estimate of its generalization ability. By systematically partitioning the dataset into multiple folds and training the model on various combinations of these folds, cross-validation reduces bias and enhances the robustness of performance estimation. It is widely used in practice for hyperparameter tuning, model selection, and assessing the predictive accuracy of machine learning models.

Evaluation Metrics:

Metrics measure the performance of models based on specific criteria, such as accuracy, precision, recall, F1 score, ROC-AUC score, mean squared error (MSE), and mean absolute error (MAE).

Evaluation metrics are quantitative measures used to assess the performance of machine learning models. These metrics provide insights into how well the model is performing on the task at hand, whether it's classification, regression, or clustering. Choosing the appropriate evaluation metrics depends on the nature of the problem and the desired outcome.

Classification Evaluation Metrics:

1. **Accuracy:** Accuracy measures the proportion of correctly classified instances out of all instances. It is calculated as the ratio of the number of correct predictions to the total number of predictions.

   $Accuracy = TP + TN + FP + FNTP + TN$

   ○ **Example:** In a binary classification problem where we want to predict whether an email is spam or not, accuracy tells us the percentage of correctly classified emails (spam or non-spam) out of all emails.

2. **Precision:** Precision measures the proportion of true positive predictions among all positive predictions made by the model. It focuses on minimizing false positives.

   $Precision = TP + FPTP$

   ○ **Example:** In a medical diagnosis scenario, precision tells us the percentage of correctly diagnosed positive cases (actual positive cases out of all predicted positive cases).

3. **Recall (Sensitivity):** Recall measures the proportion of true positive predictions among all actual positive instances in the dataset. It focuses on minimizing false negatives.

   $Recall = TP + FNTP$

- ○ **Example:** In a disease detection scenario, recall tells us the percentage of correctly identified positive cases (actual positive cases out of all actual positive cases).

4. **F1 Score:** The F1 score is the harmonic mean of precision and recall. It provides a balanced measure of a model's performance by taking into account both false positives and false negatives.
$F1\ Score = Precision + Recall 2 \times Precision \times Recall$

- ○ **Example:** In scenarios where precision and recall are both important, such as fraud detection, the F1 score provides a single metric to evaluate the model's performance.

Regression Evaluation Metrics:

1. **Mean Squared Error (MSE):** MSE measures the average squared difference between the predicted values and the actual values. It penalizes larger errors more heavily.
$2MSE = n1\Sigma i = 1 n(y_i - y\hat{}i)2$

- ○ **Example:** In predicting house prices, MSE measures the average squared difference between the predicted prices and the actual prices of houses.

2. **Mean Absolute Error (MAE):** MAE measures the average absolute difference between the predicted values and the actual values. It is less sensitive to outliers compared to MSE.
$|MAE = n1\Sigma i = 1 n|y_i - y\hat{}i|$

- ○ **Example:** In predicting student exam scores, MAE measures the average absolute difference between the predicted scores and the actual scores.

Clustering Evaluation Metrics:

1. **Silhouette Score:** Silhouette score measures how similar an object is to its own cluster compared to other clusters. It ranges from -1 to 1, where a higher score indicates better clustering.
    - **Example:** In customer segmentation, a higher silhouette score suggests that the clusters are well-separated and the objects within each cluster are similar to each other.
2. **Davies-Bouldin Index:** Davies-Bouldin index measures the average similarity between each cluster and its most similar cluster, where lower values indicate better clustering.
    - **Example:** In market basket analysis, a lower Davies-Bouldin index suggests that the clusters represent distinct groups of products with minimal overlap.

Evaluation metrics play a crucial role in assessing the performance of machine learning models across different tasks, including classification, regression, and clustering. By choosing appropriate evaluation metrics based on the problem at hand, practitioners can gain valuable insights into model performance and make informed decisions regarding model selection, hyperparameter tuning, and overall model improvement.

2. Hyperparameter Tuning:

Hyperparameters are configuration settings that control the learning process of machine learning algorithms. Hyperparameter tuning involves optimizing these settings to improve model performance and generalization.

Key Techniques:

Grid Search:

Exhaustively searches a predefined hyperparameter grid to find the optimal combination of hyperparameters. It is computationally expensive but guarantees finding the best solution within the search space.

Grid search is a systematic method for hyperparameter tuning in machine learning. It involves defining a grid of hyperparameter values and exhaustively searching through all possible combinations to find the optimal set of hyperparameters that yield the best model performance.

Explanation:

- **Grid of Hyperparameters:** In grid search, a predefined grid is created, where each dimension represents a hyperparameter to be tuned, and each point in the grid represents a specific combination of hyperparameter values.
- **Exhaustive Search:** Grid search iterates through all possible combinations of hyperparameters within the defined grid. For each combination, a model is trained and evaluated using cross-validation or a separate validation set.
- **Evaluation Criterion:** The performance of each model is evaluated using a chosen evaluation metric, such as accuracy, precision, recall, F1 score, mean squared error (MSE), or mean absolute error (MAE).
- **Selection of Best Hyperparameters:** After evaluating all combinations, the set of hyperparameters that results in the highest performance metric is selected as the optimal configuration for the model.

Example:

Consider a classification problem where we aim to build a support vector machine (SVM) classifier to predict whether a bank loan applicant will default or not based on features such as income, credit score, and loan amount.

- **Step 1: Define Hyperparameter Grid:**
  - Define a grid of hyperparameters to tune:
    - Kernel type: {'linear', 'rbf', 'poly'}
    - C (regularization parameter): {0.1, 1, 10}
    - Gamma (kernel coefficient for 'rbf' and 'poly' kernels): {0.01, 0.1, 1}

- **Step 2: Grid Search:**
    - Perform grid search by training and evaluating SVM models with each combination of hyperparameters.
    - For example, one combination might be (kernel='linear', C=1), another might be (kernel='rbf', C=10, gamma=0.1), and so on.
- **Step 3: Model Evaluation:**
    - Evaluate each model's performance using cross-validation or a validation set.
    - Compute the chosen evaluation metric (e.g., accuracy, F1 score) for each combination of hyperparameters.
- **Step 4: Select Best Hyperparameters:**
    - Choose the combination of hyperparameters that yields the highest performance metric as the optimal configuration for the SVM model.

Advantages of Grid Search:

1. **Comprehensive Search:** Grid search systematically explores all possible combinations of hyperparameters, ensuring that no promising configurations are overlooked.
2. **Easy Implementation:** Grid search is straightforward to implement and understand, making it accessible even to beginners in machine learning.
3. **Reproducibility:** Since grid search follows a predefined grid of hyperparameters, the process is reproducible, allowing for easy replication of results.

Limitations of Grid Search:

1. **Computational Cost:** Grid search can be computationally expensive, especially when dealing with a large number of hyperparameters or a wide range of values for each hyperparameter.

2. **Curse of Dimensionality:** As the number of hyperparameters and their possible values increases, the size of the search space grows exponentially, leading to longer search times.

Grid search is a powerful technique for hyperparameter tuning in machine learning, allowing practitioners to systematically search through a predefined grid of hyperparameters to find the optimal configuration for their models. While computationally intensive, grid search provides a comprehensive and reliable method for improving model performance and generalization across various machine learning tasks.

Random Search:

Randomly samples hyperparameters from predefined distributions and evaluates their performance. While less computationally intensive than grid search, it may not find the optimal solution but often discovers good hyperparameter configurations more efficiently.

Random search is a hyperparameter tuning technique that involves randomly sampling hyperparameter values from specified distributions rather than exhaustively searching through all possible combinations. It offers an efficient alternative to grid search, particularly when the hyperparameter search space is large.

Explanation:

- **Random Sampling:** In random search, hyperparameter values are randomly sampled from predefined distributions for each iteration of the search. This random sampling allows for a more diverse exploration of the hyperparameter space.
- **Flexibility:** Unlike grid search, which explores a pre-defined grid of hyperparameters, random search does not rely on a predefined grid. Instead, it allows for a flexible search across the hyperparameter space, which can be advantageous in high-dimensional spaces.

- **Efficiency:** Random search tends to be more efficient than grid search, especially in high-dimensional search spaces. By randomly sampling hyperparameters, random search can quickly identify promising regions of the search space without the need to exhaustively evaluate all possible combinations.
- **Parallelization:** Random search lends itself well to parallelization, as each iteration is independent of the others. This allows for efficient utilization of computational resources, speeding up the hyperparameter tuning process.

Example:

Consider a deep learning task where we aim to train a convolutional neural network (CNN) for image classification. We want to tune the learning rate and dropout rate hyperparameters.

- **Step 1: Define Hyperparameter Distributions:**
    - Specify distributions for each hyperparameter:
        - Learning rate (lr): Uniform distribution between 0.0001 and 0.1.
        - Dropout rate (dropout): Uniform distribution between 0.1 and 0.5.
- **Step 2: Random Search:**
    - Randomly sample hyperparameter values from the specified distributions for each iteration of the search.
    - For example, one iteration might sample lr=0.001 and dropout=0.3, another might sample lr=0.05 and dropout=0.4, and so on.
- **Step 3: Model Training and Evaluation:**
    - Train a CNN model with each sampled hyperparameter configuration.
    - Evaluate the model's performance using cross-validation or a validation set.
- **Step 4: Select Best Hyperparameters:**

- Choose the hyperparameter configuration that results in the best performance metric (e.g., validation accuracy) as the optimal set of hyperparameters.

Advantages of Random Search:

1. **Efficiency:** Random search can efficiently explore the hyperparameter space, particularly in high-dimensional spaces, without the need for exhaustive search.
2. **Flexibility:** Random search allows for a flexible exploration of the hyperparameter space, enabling the discovery of promising hyperparameter configurations.
3. **Parallelization:** Random search can be easily parallelized, allowing for concurrent evaluation of multiple hyperparameter configurations and efficient use of computational resources.

Limitations of Random Search:

1. **No Guarantee of Optimality:** Random search does not guarantee finding the optimal hyperparameters, as it relies on random sampling. However, it often identifies high-performing configurations efficiently.
2. **Uneven Exploration:** Random search may allocate more search effort to less promising regions of the hyperparameter space, potentially missing important regions of high performance.

Random search is a versatile and efficient hyperparameter tuning technique that offers advantages over exhaustive search methods like grid search. By randomly sampling hyperparameters from specified distributions, random search can efficiently explore high-dimensional search spaces and identify promising hyperparameter configurations for machine learning models. While not guaranteed to find the optimal solution, random search is a valuable tool in the machine learning practitioner's toolkit for model optimization.

Bayesian Optimization:

Uses probabilistic models to model the objective function and iteratively select hyperparameters based on their expected improvement. It efficiently explores the search space and converges to optimal solutions with fewer evaluations compared to grid and random search.

3. **Practical Examples:**

Example 1: Classification Task: Suppose you're working on a binary classification problem to predict whether emails are spam or not. After splitting your data into training, validation, and test sets, you train a logistic regression model and evaluate its performance using precision, recall, and F1 score. To improve model performance, you perform hyperparameter tuning using grid search to optimize the regularization parameter and achieve better classification accuracy.

Example 2: Regression Task: In a housing price prediction task, you train a random forest regression model to estimate house prices based on various features such as location, size, and amenities. Using k-fold cross-validation, you assess the model's performance using mean squared error (MSE). To optimize the random forest hyperparameters, you apply Bayesian optimization to find the optimal number of trees, maximum depth, and minimum samples split, resulting in a more accurate and reliable prediction model.

Cross-Validation Techniques:

Cross-validation is a fundamental technique used to assess the performance of machine learning models and to tune hyperparameters. It involves partitioning the dataset into multiple subsets, training the model on a subset of the data, and evaluating its performance on the remaining subset. Various cross-validation techniques exist, each with its own advantages and suitability for different scenarios.

1. K-Fold Cross-Validation:

In K-fold cross-validation, the dataset is divided into K equal-sized folds. The model is trained K times, each time using K-1 folds for training and the remaining fold for validation. The performance metrics are then averaged across the K iterations to obtain a single estimate of the model's performance.

Example:

Consider a dataset containing housing prices, and we want to build a regression model to predict house prices based on various features. We perform 5-fold cross-validation on the dataset:

- We divide the dataset into 5 equal-sized folds.
- For each iteration, we train the model on 4 folds and validate it on the remaining fold.
- We repeat this process 5 times, each time using a different fold as the validation set.
- Finally, we average the performance metrics, such as mean squared error (MSE), across the 5 iterations to obtain an overall estimate of the model's performance.

2. Stratified K-Fold Cross-Validation:

Stratified K-fold cross-validation is particularly useful for classification problems with imbalanced class distributions. It ensures that each fold has a similar distribution of target classes as the original dataset. This helps to mitigate the risk of biased model evaluation.

Example:

In a binary classification problem where the target variable is imbalanced (e.g., 80% negative class and 20% positive class), stratified K-fold cross-validation ensures that each fold maintains the same class distribution as the original dataset.

3. Leave-One-Out Cross-Validation (LOOCV):

Leave-One-Out Cross-Validation (LOOCV) is a special case of K-fold cross-validation where K is equal to the number of samples in the dataset. In each iteration, one sample is held out as the validation set, and the model is trained on the remaining data. This process is repeated for each sample in the dataset, resulting in N iterations (N being the number of samples).

Example:

In a dataset with 100 samples, LOOCV involves training and evaluating the model 100 times, each time leaving out one sample for validation and using the remaining 99 samples for training. The performance metrics are then averaged across the 100 iterations to obtain an overall estimate of the model's performance.

4. Time Series Cross-Validation:

Time series cross-validation is specifically designed for time series data, where the temporal order of observations is critical. It involves splitting the dataset into training and validation sets based on time, ensuring that the model is evaluated on future time periods.

Example:

In financial forecasting, where stock prices are predicted based on historical data, time series cross-validation ensures that the model is trained on past data and evaluated on future data. This helps to simulate real-world deployment scenarios where the model needs to make predictions on unseen data.

Cross-validation techniques are essential for robust model evaluation and hyperparameter tuning in machine learning. By partitioning the dataset into multiple subsets and systematically training and evaluating the model on different combinations of these subsets, cross-validation provides a reliable estimate of the model's performance and helps to identify the optimal hyperparameters. The choice of cross-validation technique depends on the nature of the data, the problem at hand, and the desired outcome.

Evaluation Metrics for Classification and Regression:

Evaluation metrics are essential tools for assessing the performance of machine learning models in both classification and regression tasks. These metrics quantify how well a model predicts outcomes compared to the ground truth, enabling practitioners to make informed decisions about model selection and optimization. Here, we'll explore commonly used evaluation metrics for both classification and regression tasks, along with examples illustrating their usage.

Evaluation Metrics for Classification:

1. **Accuracy:**
   - Definition: Accuracy measures the proportion of correctly classified instances out of all instances.
   - Formula: $Accuracy = TP + TN + FP + FNTP + TN$
   - Example: In a binary classification task for detecting fraudulent transactions, accuracy represents the percentage of correctly classified transactions (both fraudulent and non-fraudulent) out of all transactions.

2. **Precision:**
   - Definition: Precision measures the proportion of true positive predictions among all positive predictions made by the model.
   - Formula: $Precision = TP + FPTP$
   - Example: In medical diagnosis for identifying patients with a particular disease, precision indicates the percentage of correctly identified positive cases (actual positives out of all predicted positives).

3. **Recall (Sensitivity):**
   - Definition: Recall measures the proportion of true positive predictions among all actual positive instances in the dataset.

- Formula: *Recall=TP+FNTP*
- Example: In email spam detection, recall denotes the percentage of correctly identified spam emails (actual spam emails out of all actual spam emails).

4. **F1 Score:**
   - Definition: The F1 score is the harmonic mean of precision and recall, providing a balanced measure of a model's performance.
   - Formula: *F1 Score=Precision+Recall2×Precision×Recall*
   - Example: In sentiment analysis for classifying movie reviews as positive or negative, the F1 score represents the model's ability to balance precision and recall in identifying positive and negative reviews.

Evaluation Metrics for Regression:

1. **Mean Squared Error (MSE):**
   - Definition: MSE measures the average squared difference between the predicted values and the actual values.
   - Formula: *2MSE=n1Σi=1n(yi−y^i)2*
   - Example: In predicting house prices based on features like area and location, MSE quantifies the average squared deviation between the predicted prices and the actual prices of houses.

2. **Mean Absolute Error (MAE):**
   - Definition: MAE measures the average absolute difference between the predicted values and the actual values.
   - Formula: *MAE=n1Σi=1n|yi−y^i|*
   - Example: In forecasting stock prices, MAE indicates the average absolute deviation between the predicted prices and the actual prices of stocks.

3. **Root Mean Squared Error (RMSE):**

- ○ Definition: RMSE is the square root of the MSE, providing a measure of the typical magnitude of the errors.
- ○ Formula: $RMSE = \sqrt{MSE}$
- ○ Example: In weather forecasting, RMSE represents the typical magnitude of errors between the predicted and observed temperatures.

4. **R-squared (R^2) Score:**

- ○ Definition: R-squared measures the proportion of the variance in the dependent variable that is predictable from the independent variables.
- ○ Formula: $R2 = 1 - \frac{SS_{tot}}{SS_{res}}$
- ○ Example: In predicting students' exam scores based on study hours and previous grades, R-squared indicates the proportion of variance in exam scores explained by the model.

Evaluation metrics play a crucial role in assessing the performance of machine learning models in both classification and regression tasks. By choosing appropriate metrics based on the nature of the problem and the desired outcome, practitioners can gain valuable insights into model performance and make informed decisions about model selection, hyperparameter tuning, and overall model improvement.

Hyperparameter Optimization:

Hyperparameter optimization is a crucial step in the machine learning pipeline that involves finding the best set of hyperparameters for a given model to optimize its performance. Hyperparameters are parameters that are not learned by the model during training but are set prior to training and affect the model's behavior and performance

1. **Grid Search:**

Explanation:

- **Method:** Grid search exhaustively searches through a manually specified subset of the hyperparameter space.
- **Process:** It constructs a grid of hyperparameter values and evaluates the model performance for each combination of hyperparameters.
- **Selection:** The combination of hyperparameters that yields the best performance metric (e.g., accuracy, F1 score) is selected.
- **Example:** In a support vector machine (SVM) model, hyperparameters such as the choice of kernel (linear, polynomial, radial basis function), regularization parameter (C), and kernel coefficient (gamma) can be tuned using grid search.

2. Random Search:

Explanation:

- **Method:** Random search randomly samples hyperparameter values from predefined distributions.
- **Process:** It iteratively selects random combinations of hyperparameters and evaluates the model performance.
- **Selection:** The combination of hyperparameters that yields the best performance metric is chosen.
- **Example:** In a deep neural network (DNN) model, hyperparameters such as learning rate, dropout rate, and batch size can be tuned using random search.

3. Bayesian Optimization:

Explanation:

- **Method:** Bayesian optimization models the objective function (model performance) as a probabilistic surrogate model and iteratively selects hyperparameter values to minimize/maximize this function.

- **Process:** It balances exploration and exploitation by iteratively selecting hyperparameters based on the surrogate model and the acquisition function.
- **Selection:** The hyperparameter values that optimize the objective function are chosen.
- **Example:** In a gradient boosting machine (GBM) model, hyperparameters such as the number of trees, tree depth, and learning rate can be optimized using Bayesian optimization.

4. Evolutionary Algorithms:

Explanation:

- **Method:** Evolutionary algorithms mimic the process of natural selection to evolve a population of candidate solutions (sets of hyperparameters) over multiple generations.
- **Process:** It involves generating an initial population of candidate solutions, evaluating their performance, selecting the fittest solutions, and applying genetic operators (e.g., mutation, crossover) to produce offspring for the next generation.
- **Selection:** The best-performing candidate solution(s) after a predetermined number of generations are selected.
- **Example:** In a random forest model, hyperparameters such as the number of trees, maximum depth of trees, and minimum samples per leaf can be optimized using evolutionary algorithms.

5. Gradient-Based Optimization:

Explanation:

- **Method:** Gradient-based optimization uses gradient descent or its variants to iteratively update hyperparameters based on the gradients of the performance metric with respect to the hyper-parameters.

- **Process:** It computes the gradients of the performance metric using backpropagation and updates the hyperparameters in the direction that minimizes/maximizes the metric.
- **Selection:** The hyperparameters that minimize/maximize the performance metric are chosen.
- **Example:** In a neural network model, hyperparameters such as learning rate and momentum can be optimized using gradient-based optimization techniques like Adam or stochastic gradient descent (SGD) with momentum.

Hyperparameter optimization is essential for improving the performance of machine learning models and achieving better generalization on unseen data. By systematically exploring the hyperparameter space using techniques such as grid search, random search, Bayesian optimization, evolutionary algorithms, and gradient-based optimization, practitioners can fine-tune their models to achieve optimal performance for various tasks and datasets. The choice of hyperparameter optimization technique depends on factors such as the size of the hyperparameter space, computational resources, and the desired level of optimization.

Conclusion:

Model evaluation and hyperparameter tuning are essential steps in the machine learning workflow to ensure the development of accurate and robust predictive models. By carefully assessing model performance using appropriate evaluation metrics and optimizing hyperparameters using techniques such as grid search, random search, or Bayesian optimization, practitioners can improve model generalization and achieve better results on unseen data. Practical examples demonstrate the importance of these processes in various machine learning tasks, from classification and regression to more complex problems. Continued research and innovation in model evaluation and hyperparameter tuning techniques contribute to advancing the field of machine learning and enabling the development of more effective and efficient predictive models.

Chapter 10: Real-world Applications and Case Studies

Top of Form

Machine learning algorithms have found widespread applications across various industries, revolutionizing processes, optimizing operations, and unlocking new insights from data.

1. Healthcare:

Application: Predictive Analytics for Disease Diagnosis and Prognosis

- **Case Study:** Using machine learning algorithms, healthcare providers can analyze patient data, including medical history, genetic information, and diagnostic tests, to predict disease risk and prognosis accurately. For example, researchers at Stanford University developed a deep learning model that predicts the onset of diabetic retinopathy using retinal images, enabling early intervention and prevention of vision loss.

2. Finance:

Application: Fraud Detection and Risk Management

- **Case Study:** Financial institutions employ machine learning techniques to detect fraudulent transactions and mitigate risks effectively. For instance, PayPal utilizes machine learning algorithms to analyze transaction patterns, detect anomalies, and prevent fraudulent activities. By continuously learning from new data, these models adapt to evolving fraud patterns, enhancing security and protecting users' financial assets.

3. E-commerce:

Application: Personalized Recommendations and Customer Segmentation

- **Case Study:** E-commerce platforms leverage machine learning algorithms to provide personalized product recommendations and segment customers based on their preferences and behavior. Amazon's recommendation system analyzes users' browsing history, purchase patterns, and demographic information to suggest relevant products, thereby improving user engagement and driving sales.

4. Manufacturing:

Application: Predictive Maintenance and Quality Control

- **Case Study:** Manufacturing companies deploy machine learning models for predictive maintenance to anticipate equipment failures and minimize downtime. General Electric (GE) implemented predictive maintenance algorithms in its aircraft engines, analyzing sensor data to identify potential issues before they escalate into costly failures. By predicting maintenance needs accurately, GE reduced maintenance costs and improved operational efficiency.

5. Transportation:

Application: Traffic Prediction and Route Optimization

- **Case Study:** Ride-sharing companies like Uber and Lyft use machine learning algorithms to predict demand, optimize driver allocation, and minimize passenger wait times. By analyzing historical ride data, traffic patterns, and external factors like weather and events, these platforms dynamically adjust pricing and routing to meet user demand efficiently.

6. Marketing:

Application: Customer Segmentation and Targeted Advertising

- **Case Study:** Marketing firms leverage machine learning techniques to segment customers based on their demographics, preferences, and buying behavior, enabling targeted advertising campaigns. Coca-Cola, for example, used machine learning algorithms to analyze social media data and identify trends and sentiments among its customers. This insight guided the development of personalized marketing strategies tailored to different consumer segments.

Image Recognition and Classification:

Image recognition and classification have emerged as pivotal applications of machine learning, enabling computers to interpret and analyze visual data. From identifying objects in photos to diagnosing medical conditions from medical images, machine learning algorithms have revolutionized various domains. Below are some real-world applications and case studies showcasing the practical use of image recognition and classification technologies.

1. Healthcare:

Application: Medical Image Analysis for Diagnostics

- **Case Study:** In medical imaging, machine learning algorithms aid in the diagnosis and detection of diseases from medical images such as X-rays, MRIs, and CT scans. For example, researchers at Stanford University developed a deep learning model called CheXNet, which accurately detects pneumonia and other thoracic diseases from chest X-rays. This technology assists radiologists in interpreting images more efficiently, leading to improved patient outcomes and faster diagnoses.

2. Retail:

Application: Product Recognition and Inventory Management

- **Case Study:** Retailers utilize image recognition technology to automate inventory management and streamline operations. For instance, Amazon Go stores employ computer vision algorithms to track customers' movements and purchases without the need for checkout lines or cashiers. Cameras installed throughout the store capture images of products, and machine learning models recognize items as customers take them off the shelves, allowing for seamless checkout experiences and real-time inventory tracking.

3. Autonomous Vehicles:

Application: Object Detection and Scene Understanding

- **Case Study:** Self-driving cars rely on image recognition and classification algorithms to perceive their surroundings and make informed decisions. Companies like Tesla, Waymo, and Uber use deep learning models to identify pedestrians, vehicles, traffic signs, and other objects in real-time from camera feeds. By analyzing and interpreting visual data, autonomous vehicles navigate safely, avoid obstacles, and adhere to traffic rules, paving the way for safer and more efficient transportation systems.

4. Security and Surveillance:

Application: Facial Recognition and Biometric Authentication

- **Case Study:** Facial recognition technology is widely employed in security and surveillance systems for identifying individuals and enhancing security measures. Law enforcement agencies, airports, and public facilities use facial recognition algorithms to detect and track persons of interest, prevent unauthorized access, and ensure public safety. For example, the Metropolitan Police Service in London utilizes facial recognition technology to identify suspects in crowds and enhance security during major events.

5. Agriculture:

Application: Crop Monitoring and Disease Detection

- **Case Study:** In agriculture, image recognition technology assists farmers in monitoring crop health, detecting pests and diseases, and optimizing agricultural practices. Companies like Agrosmart and Prospera Technologies leverage drones equipped with cameras and machine learning algorithms to capture aerial images of farmland. These images are then analyzed to identify crop health issues, monitor growth patterns, and optimize irrigation and fertilization strategies, leading to increased yields and sustainable farming practices.

Image recognition and classification technologies have myriad real-world applications across diverse industries, from healthcare and retail to autonomous vehicles and agriculture. By harnessing the power of machine learning algorithms, organizations can automate tasks, improve decision-making processes, and unlock valuable insights from visual data. As these technologies continue to advance, their impact on various sectors is expected to grow, driving innovation and transforming the way we interact with the world around us.

Sentiment Analysis:

Sentiment analysis, also known as opinion mining, is a natural language processing (NLP) technique that involves analyzing text data to determine the sentiment expressed within it. This technology enables businesses to gain insights into customer opinions, attitudes, and emotions, allowing them to make data-driven decisions and enhance customer experiences. Below are some real-world applications and case studies illustrating the practical use of sentiment analysis across different industries.

1. **Social Media Monitoring:**

Application: Brand Reputation Management

- **Case Study:** Companies use sentiment analysis to monitor social media platforms like Twitter, Facebook, and Instagram to gauge public sentiment towards their brands and products. For example, Coca-Cola utilizes sentiment analysis tools to track mentions of its brand across social media channels in real-time. By analyzing the sentiment of user comments and posts, Coca-Cola gains valuable insights into consumer perceptions, identifies emerging trends, and responds promptly to customer feedback, thereby safeguarding its brand reputation.

2. **Customer Feedback Analysis:**

Application: Product and Service Improvement

- **Case Study:** Businesses leverage sentiment analysis to analyze customer feedback from surveys, reviews, and customer support interactions. For instance, Airbnb employs sentiment analysis algorithms to analyze guest reviews and identify areas for improvement in its rental properties. By extracting sentiment from guest reviews, Airbnb identifies common issues, such as cleanliness or communication problems, and provides feedback to hosts, enabling them to address concerns and enhance the overall guest experience.

3. Market Research:

Application: Consumer Insights and Trend Analysis

- **Case Study:** Market research firms utilize sentiment analysis to analyze consumer opinions and sentiments towards products, brands, and trends. Nielsen, a global market research company, integrates sentiment analysis into its consumer insights platform to analyze social media conversations, online reviews, and forum discussions. By understanding consumer sentiments, Nielsen helps businesses identify emerging trends, assess brand perception, and make informed marketing decisions to stay competitive in the market.

4. Financial Analysis:

Application: Stock Market Prediction and Investment Strategies

- **Case Study:** Financial institutions use sentiment analysis to analyze news articles, social media discussions, and financial reports to gauge market sentiment and predict stock price movements. For example, Bloomberg incorporates sentiment analysis algorithms into its financial news platform to analyze news articles and social media posts for sentiment signals. By identifying positive or negative sentiment trends, traders and investors can make more informed decisions about buying or selling stocks, optimizing their investment strategies.

5. Healthcare:

Application: Patient Feedback Analysis and Healthcare Quality Assessment

- **Case Study:** Healthcare providers leverage sentiment analysis to analyze patient feedback surveys, online reviews, and patient forums to assess the quality of care and patient satisfaction levels. Mayo Clinic, a renowned healthcare organization, utilizes sentiment analysis tools to analyze patient feedback from online surveys and reviews. By identifying areas of concern and areas of excellence, Mayo Clinic continuously improves its healthcare services, enhances patient experiences, and maintains high patient satisfaction levels.

Sentiment analysis is a powerful tool that enables businesses to extract valuable insights from text data, understand customer sentiments, and make data-driven decisions across various industries. By leveraging sentiment analysis technologies, organizations can monitor brand reputation, improve products and services, identify market trends, optimize investment strategies, and enhance customer experiences. As sentiment analysis continues to evolve, its applications and impact on businesses are expected to grow, driving innovation and shaping the future of customer engagement and market intelligence.

Fraud Detection:

Fraud detection is a critical area where machine learning algorithms play a pivotal role in identifying and preventing fraudulent activities across various industries. By leveraging advanced data analytics techniques, organizations can detect anomalies, patterns, and suspicious behavior in large datasets, thereby minimizing financial losses and maintaining trust and integrity. Here are some real-world applications and case studies demonstrating the practical use of fraud detection technologies:

1. **Financial Services:**

Application: Credit Card Fraud Detection

- **Case Study:** Financial institutions deploy machine learning algorithms to detect fraudulent transactions and protect customers from unauthorized use of their credit cards. For example, Visa utilizes a combination of supervised and unsupervised learning algorithms to analyze transaction data in real-time. By detecting anomalies, unusual spending patterns, and discrepancies in transaction behavior, Visa's fraud detection system alerts customers and blocks potentially fraudulent transactions, preventing financial losses and safeguarding the integrity of the payment network.

2. **Insurance:**

Application: Insurance Claims Fraud Detection

- **Case Study:** Insurance companies employ machine learning models to detect fraudulent insurance claims and mitigate risks. For instance, Progressive Insurance utilizes predictive analytics and anomaly detection algorithms to analyze insurance claims data. By identifying suspicious patterns, inconsistencies, and fraudulent claims, Progressive reduces fraudulent payouts, improves operational efficiency, and ensures fair premiums for policyholders.

3. **E-commerce:**

Application: Online Transaction Fraud Detection

- **Case Study:** E-commerce platforms implement fraud detection systems to protect against online transaction fraud, such as account takeover, payment fraud, and identity theft. Amazon, one of the world's largest e-commerce companies, employs machine learning algorithms to analyze user behavior, transaction history, and device fingerprinting data. By detecting anomalies and fraudulent activities in real-time, Amazon prevents unauthorized transactions, mitigates financial losses, and enhances trust and security for its customers.

4. Healthcare:

Application: Healthcare Fraud Detection

- **Case Study:** Healthcare organizations utilize machine learning algorithms to identify fraudulent activities, such as billing fraud, prescription fraud, and healthcare provider fraud. For example, UnitedHealth Group employs advanced analytics and anomaly detection techniques to analyze claims data and detect fraudulent billing practices. By flagging suspicious claims, UnitedHealth Group reduces fraudulent payouts, lowers healthcare costs, and ensures compliance with regulatory requirements.

5. Telecom:

Application: Telecom Fraud Detection

- **Case Study:** Telecommunication companies leverage machine learning models to detect telecom fraud, such as call fraud, subscription fraud, and roaming fraud. Vodafone, a multinational telecommunications company, utilizes predictive analytics and pattern recognition algorithms to analyze call detail records (CDRs) and network traffic data. By identifying unusual calling patterns, SIM card swapping, and other fraudulent activities, Vodafone minimizes revenue losses, protects customer accounts, and maintains the integrity of its network.

Fraud detection is a critical component of risk management and security strategies for organizations across various industries. By leveraging machine learning algorithms, organizations can analyze vast amounts of data, detect anomalies, and identify suspicious behavior in real-time, thereby mitigating financial losses, protecting assets, and maintaining trust and integrity. As fraudsters continue to evolve their tactics, the use of advanced analytics and artificial intelligence technologies will be essential in staying ahead of emerging threats and safeguarding against fraudulent activities.

Recommendation Systems:

Recommendation systems are widely used in various industries to provide personalized recommendations to users based on their preferences, behavior, and historical data. These systems leverage machine learning algorithms to analyze user interactions, item attributes, and contextual information to suggest relevant items, products, or content. Here are some real-world applications and case studies demonstrating the practical use of recommendation systems:

1. **E-commerce:**

Application: Product Recommendations

- **Case Study:** Amazon, the world's largest online retailer, employs recommendation systems to suggest products to customers based on their browsing history, purchase behavior, and demographic information. Amazon's recommendation engine analyzes user interactions, item attributes, and transaction history to generate personalized product recommendations on its website and mobile app. By providing relevant product suggestions, Amazon enhances user experience, increases engagement, and drives sales.

2. Streaming Services:

Application: Content Recommendations

- **Case Study:** Netflix, a leading streaming service provider, utilizes recommendation systems to suggest movies and TV shows to subscribers based on their viewing history, ratings, and preferences. Netflix's recommendation engine analyzes user interactions, viewing patterns, and content metadata to generate personalized recommendations tailored to each subscriber's tastes and interests. By delivering personalized content recommendations, Netflix improves user satisfaction, retention, and subscription revenues.

3. Social Media:

Application: Friend Recommendations

- **Case Study:** Facebook, the world's largest social networking platform, employs recommendation systems to suggest friends to users based on their mutual connections, interests, and activity on the platform. Facebook's friend recommendation algorithm analyzes user profiles, social graphs, and interaction patterns to identify potential friends or acquaintances. By facilitating social connections and expanding users' social networks, Facebook enhances user engagement and interaction on its platform.

4. Music Streaming:

Application: Music Recommendations

- **Case Study:** Spotify, a popular music streaming service, utilizes recommendation systems to suggest songs, playlists, and artists to users based on their listening history, preferences, and mood. Spotify's recommendation engine analyzes user-generated playlists, listening habits, and music metadata to generate personalized recommendations tailored to each user's taste and mood. By providing curated music recommendations, Spotify enhances user satisfaction, retention, and subscription revenues.

5. Online Retail:

Application: Cross-selling and Upselling Recommendations

- **Case Study:** eBay, a global online marketplace, employs recommendation systems to suggest complementary or higher-value products to users based on their browsing and purchasing behavior. eBay's recommendation engine analyzes user interactions, item attributes, and transaction history to generate personalized cross-selling and upselling recommendations. By offering relevant product suggestions, eBay increases average order value, conversion rates, and customer satisfaction.

Recommendation systems play a crucial role in enhancing user experience, engagement, and satisfaction across various digital platforms and services. By leveraging machine learning algorithms and data analytics techniques, organizations can deliver personalized recommendations tailored to each user's preferences, behavior, and context. As recommendation systems continue to evolve, their applications and impact on user engagement, retention, and revenue generation are expected to grow, driving innovation and reshaping the digital landscape.

Conclusion:

Machine learning technologies have transformed various industries, enabling organizations to extract valuable insights from data, automate processes, and deliver personalized experiences to customers. The real-world applications and case studies highlighted above demonstrate the diverse range of applications of machine learning across healthcare, finance, e-commerce, manufacturing, transportation, and marketing. As machine learning continues to advance, its impact on industries and society at large is poised to grow, driving innovation and reshaping business landscapes.

Chapter 11: Ethical Considerations in Machine Learning

As machine learning technologies become increasingly integrated into various aspects of society, it's crucial to address the ethical implications associated with their development, deployment, and use. Ethical considerations in machine learning encompass a wide range of issues, including bias and fairness, privacy concerns, accountability, transparency, and societal impact. Addressing these ethical considerations is essential to ensure that machine learning systems are deployed responsibly and equitably. Below are some key ethical considerations in machine learning, along with examples illustrating their importance:

1. **Bias and Fairness:**

- **Issue:** Machine learning models can inadvertently perpetuate biases present in the data used for training, leading to unfair outcomes for certain groups.
- **Example:** In 2018, it was reported that Amazon's recruiting tool developed using machine learning exhibited bias against female candidates. The algorithm was trained on historical resumes, which were predominantly from male applicants, leading to the system favoring male candidates over female candidates.

2. Privacy Concerns:

- **Issue:** Machine learning systems often require access to large amounts of personal data, raising concerns about privacy infringement and data misuse.
- **Example:** Facebook's use of user data for targeted advertising has raised significant privacy concerns. In 2018, the Cambridge Analytica scandal revealed that personal data of millions of Facebook users were harvested without their consent and used for political advertising purposes.

3. Accountability:

- **Issue:** It can be challenging to assign responsibility when machine learning systems make erroneous or harmful decisions.
- **Example:** In 2016, Microsoft's Tay chatbot, trained on Twitter data, began generating racist and offensive tweets within hours of being launched. Microsoft faced criticism for failing to adequately anticipate and prevent such behavior, highlighting the need for accountability in machine learning systems.

4. Transparency:

- **Issue:** Machine learning models often operate as black boxes, making it difficult to understand how decisions are made, leading to a lack of transparency and accountability.
- **Example:** In the criminal justice system, the use of predictive algorithms for risk assessment has raised concerns about transparency and due process. Defendants and their legal representatives may not have access to information about how these algorithms arrive at risk scores, potentially compromising defendants' rights to challenge their assessments.

5. Societal Impact:

- **Issue:** Machine learning technologies can have wide-ranging societal impacts, including job displacement, exacerbation of inequalities, and manipulation of public opinion.
- **Example:** The automation of jobs through the use of artificial intelligence and robotics has raised concerns about unemployment and income inequality. Low-skilled workers are particularly vulnerable to job displacement, leading to socioeconomic challenges in affected communities.

Addressing Ethical Considerations:

- **Data Collection and Labeling:** Ensuring diverse and representative datasets, as well as careful labeling of data to mitigate biases.
- **Model Interpretability:** Developing models that are interpretable and explainable to facilitate transparency and accountability.
- **Regulatory Oversight:** Implementing regulations and standards to govern the development and deployment of machine learning systems, such as the General Data Protection Regulation (GDPR) in the European Union.
- **Ethical Frameworks:** Adopting ethical frameworks and guidelines, such as the AI Ethics Guidelines provided by organizations like the Institute of Electrical and Electronics Engineers (IEEE) and the Association for Computing Machinery (ACM).

Bias and Fairness:

As machine learning technologies become increasingly integrated into various aspects of society, it's crucial to address the ethical implications associated with their development, deployment, and use. Ethical considerations in machine learning encompass a wide range of issues, including bias and fairness, privacy concerns, accountability, transparency, and societal impact. Addressing these ethical considerations is essential to ensure that machine learning systems are deployed responsibly and equitably. Below are some key ethical considerations in machine learning, along with examples illustrating their importance:

1. **Bias and Fairness:**

- **Issue:** Machine learning models can inadvertently perpetuate biases present in the data used for training, leading to unfair outcomes for certain groups.
- **Example:** In 2018, it was reported that Amazon's recruiting tool developed using machine learning exhibited bias against female candidates. The algorithm was trained on historical resumes, which were predominantly from male applicants, leading to the system favoring male candidates over female candidates.

2. **Privacy Concerns:**

- **Issue:** Machine learning systems often require access to large amounts of personal data, raising concerns about privacy infringement and data misuse.
- **Example:** Facebook's use of user data for targeted advertising has raised significant privacy concerns. In 2018, the Cambridge Analytica scandal revealed that personal data of millions of Facebook users were harvested without their consent and used for political advertising purposes.

3. **Accountability:**

- **Issue:** It can be challenging to assign responsibility when machine learning systems make erroneous or harmful decisions.

- **Example:** In 2016, Microsoft's Tay chatbot, trained on Twitter data, began generating racist and offensive tweets within hours of being launched. Microsoft faced criticism for failing to adequately anticipate and prevent such behavior, highlighting the need for accountability in machine learning systems.

4. Transparency:

- **Issue:** Machine learning models often operate as black boxes, making it difficult to understand how decisions are made, leading to a lack of transparency and accountability.
- **Example:** In the criminal justice system, the use of predictive algorithms for risk assessment has raised concerns about transparency and due process. Defendants and their legal representatives may not have access to information about how these algorithms arrive at risk scores, potentially compromising defendants' rights to challenge their assessments.

5. Societal Impact:

- **Issue:** Machine learning technologies can have wide-ranging societal impacts, including job displacement, exacerbation of inequalities, and manipulation of public opinion.
- **Example:** The automation of jobs through the use of artificial intelligence and robotics has raised concerns about unemployment and income inequality. Low-skilled workers are particularly vulnerable to job displacement, leading to socioeconomic challenges in affected communities.

Addressing Ethical Considerations:

- **Data Collection and Labeling:** Ensuring diverse and representative datasets, as well as careful labeling of data to mitigate biases.
- **Model Interpretability:** Developing models that are interpretable and explainable to facilitate transparency and accountability.
- **Regulatory Oversight:** Implementing regulations and standards to govern the development and deployment of machine learning systems, such as the General Data Protection Regulation (GDPR) in the European Union.
- **Ethical Frameworks:** Adopting ethical frameworks and guidelines, such as the AI Ethics Guidelines provided by organizations like the Institute of Electrical and Electronics Engineers (IEEE) and the Association for Computing Machinery (ACM).

Ethical considerations are paramount in the development and deployment of machine learning technologies. By addressing issues related to bias and fairness, privacy concerns, accountability, transparency, and societal impact, stakeholders can ensure that machine learning systems are deployed responsibly and ethically, benefiting society while minimizing harm. It is essential for developers, policymakers, and organizations to prioritize ethical considerations throughout the entire lifecycle of machine learning systems, from data collection and model development to deployment and evaluation.

Privacy and Security Concerns:

Privacy and security are paramount in the development and deployment of machine learning (ML) systems, as these technologies often involve the processing of sensitive personal data. Ensuring the privacy and security of individuals' data is essential to maintain trust, protect user rights, and mitigate potential harms. Here's an in-depth exploration of the ethical considerations related to privacy and security in machine learning, along with examples illustrating their significance:

1. Data Privacy:

- **Issue:** Machine learning algorithms typically require access to large volumes of data, including personal information, to train models effectively. However, the collection and use of sensitive data raise concerns about individuals' privacy rights and data protection.
- **Example:** Health-related applications, such as fitness trackers and medical diagnosis systems, often collect extensive data about users' physical activities, health conditions, and biometric measurements. Failure to adequately protect this data could result in privacy breaches and compromise users' confidentiality.

2. Data Security:

- **Issue:** Machine learning systems are susceptible to security threats, such as data breaches, unauthorized access, and adversarial attacks. Weaknesses in system security can lead to the unauthorized disclosure, alteration, or theft of sensitive data.
- **Example:** In 2017, Equifax, one of the largest credit reporting agencies, suffered a massive data breach that exposed the personal information of approximately 147 million consumers. The breach, caused by a vulnerability in Equifax's website application, underscored the importance of robust security measures to protect sensitive data from unauthorized access.

3. User Consent and Control:

- **Issue:** Users may not always be aware of how their data is being collected, used, and shared by machine learning systems. Lack of transparency and control over data can erode user trust and autonomy.

- **Example:** Social media platforms like Facebook have faced criticism for their handling of user data and privacy settings. Instances of unauthorized data sharing with third-party developers and changes to privacy policies without clear user consent have led to public outcry and regulatory scrutiny.

4. Algorithmic Bias and Discrimination:

- **Issue:** Biases present in training data can perpetuate discriminatory outcomes in machine learning models, leading to unfair treatment and negative consequences for certain groups.
- **Example:** Facial recognition systems have been shown to exhibit biases against certain demographic groups, particularly people of color and women. Studies have found that these systems are more likely to misclassify or misidentify individuals from underrepresented groups, raising concerns about racial and gender bias in algorithmic decision-making.

5. Adversarial Attacks:

- **Issue:** Adversarial attacks involve manipulating machine learning models by introducing small, imperceptible changes to input data to deceive or compromise their performance.
- **Example:** Researchers have demonstrated adversarial attacks against image classification systems, where slight modifications to input images can cause models to misclassify objects or produce incorrect predictions. These attacks highlight vulnerabilities in machine learning models and the need for robust defenses against adversarial manipulation.

Addressing Privacy and Security Concerns:

- Implementing Privacy by Design principles to embed privacy protections into the design and development of machine learning systems.
- Adopting encryption, access controls, and secure authentication mechanisms to safeguard data during storage, processing, and transmission.
- Providing users with transparent information about data collection practices, purposes, and rights, and obtaining explicit consent for data processing activities.
- Regularly auditing and testing machine learning systems for vulnerabilities, biases, and adversarial attacks, and implementing measures to mitigate risks.

Privacy and security concerns are central to the responsible development and deployment of machine learning systems. By addressing issues related to data privacy, security vulnerabilities, user consent and control, algorithmic bias, and adversarial attacks, stakeholders can ensure that machine learning technologies respect individuals' rights, uphold ethical standards, and mitigate potential harms. Upholding privacy and security principles is essential to foster trust, protect user data, and promote the responsible use of machine learning in society.

Transparency and Accountability:

Transparency and accountability are critical aspects of ethical machine learning practices. They ensure that stakeholders understand how machine learning models make decisions, how they are trained, and who is responsible for their outcomes. By promoting transparency and accountability, organizations can build trust with users, mitigate potential biases, and address concerns related to fairness and interpretability. Here's an in-depth exploration of the ethical considerations related to transparency and accountability in machine learning, along with examples illustrating their significance:

1. Model Transparency:

- **Issue:** Machine learning models often operate as "black boxes," making it challenging to understand how they arrive at their decisions. Lack of transparency can lead to mistrust among users and stakeholders.
- **Example:** Google's PageRank algorithm, used for ranking web pages in search results, is an example of a transparent machine learning model. Google provides insights into how PageRank works, including factors such as link quality, relevance, and user engagement, fostering trust and understanding among users.

2. Explainability and Interpretability:

- **Issue:** Machine learning models should be interpretable, allowing users to understand the factors influencing their decisions. Lack of explainability can hinder users' ability to assess the fairness and validity of model outcomes.
- **Example:** In the context of credit scoring, a transparent machine learning model would provide explanations for why a particular applicant was approved or denied credit. This transparency enables applicants to understand the factors influencing their creditworthiness and challenge decisions if necessary.

3. Bias and Fairness:

- **Issue:** Lack of transparency in machine learning models can obscure biases present in training data, leading to unfair outcomes for certain groups. Transparent models allow stakeholders to identify and address biases effectively.
- **Example:** In the recruitment process, a transparent machine learning model would reveal any biases present in the data used to train the model. For instance, if historical hiring data shows a

bias towards certain demographic groups, stakeholders can take corrective measures to ensure fairer recruitment practices.

4. Accountability and Responsibility:

- **Issue:** It's essential to establish clear lines of accountability for machine learning systems to ensure that responsible parties are held accountable for their decisions and outcomes.
- **Example:** In autonomous vehicles, the manufacturer, developer, and operator share responsibility for the vehicle's actions. Transparent systems allow stakeholders to trace decision-making processes back to responsible parties in the event of accidents or errors.

5. Auditing and Validation:

- **Issue:** Transparent machine learning models should undergo regular auditing and validation to ensure their accuracy, fairness, and compliance with ethical standards and regulations.
- **Example:** Financial institutions use transparent machine learning models for credit risk assessment. These models are subject to regular audits and validations to verify their compliance with regulatory requirements and to assess their fairness and accuracy in predicting creditworthiness.

Addressing Transparency and Accountability:

- Implementing model documentation and explanation techniques, such as providing feature importance scores or decision rationale.
- Adopting open-source and collaborative development practices to facilitate peer review and scrutiny of machine learning models.

- Establishing clear policies and guidelines for data collection, model development, and decision-making processes to promote accountability.
- Engaging with stakeholders, including users, policymakers, and advocacy groups, to solicit feedback and ensure transparency in machine learning practices.

Transparency and accountability are essential pillars of ethical machine learning. By promoting transparency in model operations and decision-making processes and establishing clear lines of accountability, organizations can build trust with users, mitigate biases, and ensure fairness and accountability in machine learning systems. Upholding transparency and accountability principles is crucial for fostering trust, ensuring fairness, and promoting responsible use of machine learning technologies in society.

Conclusion:

Ethical considerations are paramount in the development and deployment of machine learning technologies. By addressing issues related to bias and fairness, privacy concerns, accountability, transparency, and societal impact, stakeholders can ensure that machine learning systems are deployed responsibly and ethically, benefiting society while minimizing harm. It is essential for developers, policymakers, and organizations to prioritize ethical considerations throughout the entire lifecycle of machine learning systems, from data collection and model development to deployment and evaluation.

Chapter 12: Future Trends in Machine Learning

Machine learning (ML) continues to evolve rapidly, driven by advancements in technology, data availability, and computational power. As we look to the future, several trends are poised to shape the landscape of machine learning, influencing research, applications, and industry practices. Here's an in-depth exploration of some future trends in machine learning, along with examples illustrating their potential impact:

1. **Federated Learning:**

- **Overview:** Federated learning enables model training across distributed devices or data sources while preserving data privacy. Instead of centralizing data on a server, federated learning allows models to be trained locally on user devices, with only model updates aggregated centrally.
- **Example:** Google's Federated Learning of Cohorts (FLoC) is a privacy-preserving advertising technology that enables targeted advertising without exposing individual user data. FLoC uses federated learning to train a cohort-based model on users'

devices, ensuring user privacy while still delivering personalized ad experiences.

2. Continual Learning:

- **Overview:** Continual learning focuses on developing machine learning models that can adapt and learn from new data over time without forgetting previously acquired knowledge. This capability is crucial for handling evolving datasets and dynamic environments.
- **Example:** In autonomous driving, continual learning enables vehicles to adapt to changing road conditions, new traffic patterns, and unexpected scenarios while retaining knowledge learned from past experiences. Continual learning ensures that autonomous vehicles remain capable and safe as they encounter new situations on the road.

3. Explainable AI (XAI):

- **Overview:** Explainable AI aims to enhance the transparency and interpretability of machine learning models, allowing users to understand how decisions are made and trust the outcomes. XAI techniques provide insights into model predictions, feature importance, and decision rationale.
- **Example:** In healthcare, explainable AI is crucial for interpreting and validating predictions made by medical diagnosis models. By providing explanations for diagnosis recommendations, XAI helps healthcare professionals understand and trust AI-driven diagnoses, leading to more informed decision-making and better patient care.

4. AutoML and Automated Machine Learning:

- **Overview:** AutoML refers to the automation of machine learning model development processes, including feature engineering, algorithm selection, hyperparameter tuning, and model deployment. Automated ML tools aim to democratize machine learning by making it more accessible to users with varying levels of expertise.
- **Example:** Google's Cloud AutoML platform provides a suite of tools for building custom machine learning models without extensive programming or data science expertise. Users can leverage AutoML to develop models for image classification, natural language processing, and structured data analysis, accelerating the model development process and reducing the barrier to entry for ML adoption.

5. Reinforcement Learning in Real-world Applications:

- **Overview:** Reinforcement learning (RL) has shown remarkable progress in solving complex decision-making problems, such as game playing and robotics control. In the future, RL is expected to find broader applications in domains such as finance, healthcare, and resource management.
- **Example:** DeepMind's AlphaFold is an RL-based system that predicts protein structures with remarkable accuracy. By leveraging RL algorithms, AlphaFold has revolutionized protein folding prediction, enabling advancements in drug discovery, disease understanding, and protein engineering.

6. Ethical AI and Responsible AI Practices:

- **Overview:** As machine learning systems become more pervasive, there is growing awareness of the ethical and societal implications of AI technologies. Future trends will emphasize the development and adoption of ethical AI frameworks, responsible

AI practices, and regulatory guidelines to ensure fairness, accountability, and transparency in AI systems.

- **Example:** The European Union's proposed AI regulations aim to establish clear rules and standards for AI systems, including requirements for transparency, accountability, and human oversight. By enforcing ethical AI principles, these regulations seek to mitigate risks associated with AI deployment and protect individuals' rights and well-being.

Explainable AI:

Explainable AI (XAI) is a rapidly evolving field within machine learning that focuses on developing models and techniques to provide transparent and interpretable insights into the decision-making process of AI systems. As machine learning models become increasingly complex and pervasive across various domains, the need for explainability becomes paramount to ensure trust, accountability, and fairness. Here's an in-depth exploration of the future trends in Explainable AI, along with examples illustrating their potential impact:

1. **Model-specific Explainability Techniques:**

- **Overview:** Future trends in Explainable AI will likely see the development of model-specific explainability techniques tailored to different types of machine learning models, including deep neural networks, tree-based models, and ensemble methods. These techniques aim to provide insights into how specific model architectures and algorithms arrive at their predictions.
- **Example:** For deep neural networks, techniques such as Layer-wise Relevance Propagation (LRP) and Gradient-weighted Class Activation Mapping (Grad-CAM) provide insights into feature importance and activation patterns at different layers of the

network. These techniques help users understand which parts of the input data are most influential in driving model predictions.

2. Interactive and Context-aware Explanations:

- **Overview:** Future trends in XAI will focus on providing interactive and context-aware explanations that adapt to users' needs and preferences. Interactive explanations allow users to explore model predictions and decision pathways interactively, while context-aware explanations take into account the broader context in which predictions are made.
- **Example:** In healthcare, interactive XAI tools can help clinicians understand the rationale behind AI-driven diagnoses by providing real-time feedback and allowing them to query the model for additional information. Context-aware explanations may consider patient history, demographics, and clinical guidelines to provide personalized and clinically relevant insights.

3. Uncertainty Quantification and Confidence Estimation:

- **Overview:** Uncertainty quantification techniques aim to provide measures of confidence and uncertainty associated with model predictions. Future trends in XAI will likely focus on developing robust methods for estimating uncertainty and conveying confidence levels to users, particularly in high-stakes applications where decision accuracy is critical.
- **Example:** In autonomous driving, uncertainty quantification techniques can help self-driving vehicles assess the reliability of their perception systems and make safe decisions in uncertain or ambiguous situations, such as adverse weather conditions or unfamiliar environments.

4. Model Agnostic Explanations:

- **Overview:** Model-agnostic explanation techniques are designed to provide insights into the decision-making process of any machine learning model, regardless of its architecture or complexity. These techniques offer flexibility and compatibility across a wide range of models and applications.
- **Example:** LIME (Local Interpretable Model-agnostic Explanations) is a popular model-agnostic explanation technique that generates locally interpretable approximations of complex models by perturbing input data and observing the resulting changes in predictions. LIME can be applied to various types of machine learning models, including black-box models, providing transparent explanations without requiring access to model internals.

5. Ethical and Human-centered XAI:

- **Overview:** Future trends in XAI will emphasize the development of ethical and human-centered approaches to explainability, ensuring that XAI techniques prioritize user needs, values, and preferences while upholding principles of fairness, accountability, and transparency.
- **Example:** Ethical XAI frameworks may incorporate principles such as fairness, accountability, and transparency (FAT) to guide the design and implementation of XAI systems. These frameworks ensure that XAI techniques promote ethical AI practices and mitigate potential risks associated with biased or unfair model decisions.

Explainable AI is poised to play a pivotal role in shaping the future of machine learning by enhancing transparency, interpretability, and trustworthiness of AI systems. By embracing model-specific explainability techniques, interactive and context-aware explanations, uncertainty quantification methods, model-agnostic approaches, and ethical XAI frameworks, organizations can ensure that AI systems are transparent, accountable, and aligned with human values and preferences. Through continued research and innovation in XAI, the future holds promise for building AI systems that are not only intelligent but also transparent, ethical, and human-centric.

Federated Learning:

Federated learning is an emerging paradigm in machine learning that enables model training across decentralized and heterogeneous devices or data sources while preserving data privacy. As the volume of data continues to grow and privacy concerns become increasingly important, federated learning offers a promising approach to train machine learning models collaboratively without centralizing sensitive data. Here's an in-depth exploration of the future trends in federated learning, along with examples illustrating their potential impact:

1. **Decentralized Model Training:**

- **Overview:** Future trends in federated learning will likely see the proliferation of decentralized model training across a diverse range of devices, including smartphones, IoT devices, edge servers, and wearables. Decentralized training enables models to learn from data generated at the source, reducing the need for data transfer and preserving data privacy.
- **Example:** In healthcare, federated learning allows hospitals to collaboratively train machine learning models using patient data while keeping sensitive medical information local to each institution. This approach enables the development of predictive models for disease diagnosis and treatment recommendation without compromising patient privacy.

2. **Edge Computing and Federated Learning:**

- **Overview:** Edge computing platforms, equipped with computing resources and machine learning capabilities, are poised to leverage federated learning for model training and inference at the network edge. Federated learning on edge devices enables real-time data processing, low-latency model updates, and enhanced privacy and security.

- **Example:** Smart home devices equipped with edge computing capabilities can collaboratively learn user preferences and behavior patterns using federated learning techniques. By training predictive models directly on edge devices, such as smart thermostats or security cameras, users can benefit from personalized services while maintaining control over their data.

3. Cross-device Federated Learning:

- **Overview:** Cross-device federated learning enables model training across multiple devices owned by a single user, allowing models to learn from data generated on smartphones, tablets, laptops, and other personal devices. This approach enhances model performance and personalization while respecting user privacy.

- **Example:** Personalized voice assistants, such as Amazon Alexa or Google Assistant, can leverage cross-device federated learning to improve speech recognition accuracy and natural language understanding across multiple devices used by a single user. By training on data from various devices, voice assistants can adapt to users' preferences and speech patterns more effectively.

4. Privacy-preserving Federated Learning:

- **Overview:** Future trends in federated learning will prioritize privacy-preserving techniques to ensure that sensitive data remains protected during model training and aggregation. Techniques such as differential privacy, secure aggregation, and encryption enable federated learning systems to maintain privacy guarantees while aggregating model updates.

- **Example:** Financial institutions can adopt privacy-preserving federated learning techniques to develop fraud detection models without sharing individual transaction data between banks. By training models collaboratively while preserving data privacy, banks can collectively improve fraud detection capabilities without compromising customer confidentiality.

5. Federated Learning in Industry and IoT:

- **Overview:** Federated learning is expected to find widespread applications in various industries, including healthcare, finance, manufacturing, transportation, and IoT. As organizations seek to leverage data from distributed sources while respecting privacy regulations, federated learning offers a scalable and privacy-preserving approach to model training.
- **Example:** In the transportation sector, federated learning enables vehicle manufacturers to collaboratively train autonomous driving models using data collected from diverse fleets of vehicles. By sharing knowledge while keeping sensitive vehicle data local, federated learning accelerates model development and improves safety and performance across the industry.

Federated learning represents a transformative approach to machine learning that enables collaborative model training across decentralized and heterogeneous data sources while preserving privacy and security. As federated learning continues to evolve, it holds tremendous potential to drive innovation across industries, enable personalized services, and empower users with greater control over their data. By embracing federated learning techniques and applications, organizations can unlock new opportunities for collaboration, efficiency, and privacy-enhanced machine learning in the digital age.

Edge Computing and IoT:

Edge computing, coupled with the Internet of Things (IoT), is revolutionizing the landscape of machine learning by enabling real-time data processing, low-latency decision-making, and enhanced intelligence at the network edge. As the volume of IoT devices grows and the demand for real-time insights increases, edge computing and IoT are expected to play a pivotal role in shaping the future of machine learning. Here's an in-depth exploration of the future trends in edge computing and IoT within the context of machine learning, along with examples illustrating their potential impact:

1. **Edge Intelligence for Real-time Decision-making:**

   - **Overview:** Edge computing platforms, deployed close to IoT devices and sensors, enable real-time data processing and analysis at the network edge. By bringing computational resources closer to the data source, edge intelligence reduces latency and bandwidth requirements while facilitating rapid decision-making.
   - **Example:** In smart cities, edge computing facilitates real-time traffic management by processing data from IoT sensors installed at intersections, traffic lights, and roadways. Edge intelligence analyzes traffic patterns, identifies congestion points, and adjusts traffic signals in real time to optimize traffic flow and minimize delays.

2. **Distributed Machine Learning at the Edge:**

   - **Overview:** Edge computing environments support distributed machine learning algorithms that enable model training and inference directly on edge devices or local edge servers. Distributed ML at the edge leverages data proximity and reduces reliance on centralized cloud resources, making it well-suited for applications requiring low-latency and offline operation.

- **Example:** In industrial IoT (IIoT) settings, edge devices equipped with sensors and actuators monitor manufacturing processes and equipment health in real time. Distributed ML algorithms deployed at the edge analyze sensor data to predict equipment failures, optimize production schedules, and prevent costly downtime without relying on continuous cloud connectivity.

3. Federated Learning in Edge Environments:

- **Overview:** Federated learning extends to edge computing environments, allowing models to be trained collaboratively across distributed edge devices while preserving data privacy. Federated learning at the edge leverages local data sources to train models tailored to specific edge environments, such as smart buildings, autonomous vehicles, and wearable devices.
- **Example:** In healthcare, wearable devices equipped with health sensors collect physiological data from patients, such as heart rate, blood pressure, and activity levels. Federated learning enables models to be trained directly on edge devices, providing personalized health insights while ensuring patient data remains private and secure.

4. Edge-Cloud Synergy for Scalable ML:

- **Overview:** Edge computing complements cloud-based machine learning by offloading computation-intensive tasks to local edge devices, reducing cloud dependency and improving scalability and efficiency. Edge-cloud synergy enables seamless integration between edge and cloud resources, allowing organizations to leverage the strengths of both environments for ML applications.

- **Example:** In retail, edge computing enhances customer experience by enabling personalized recommendations and real-time inventory management. Edge devices installed in stores analyze customer behavior, product interactions, and inventory levels to deliver targeted promotions and optimize stock replenishment, while cloud-based analytics provide insights across multiple store locations.

5. AI-powered Edge Security and Anomaly Detection:

- **Overview:** Edge computing platforms integrate AI-powered security mechanisms for detecting and mitigating cybersecurity threats in real time. AI-driven anomaly detection algorithms analyze network traffic, device behavior, and system logs to identify suspicious activities and respond proactively to security breaches at the network edge.
- **Example:** In smart homes, edge devices equipped with AI-powered security cameras and sensors monitor premises for unauthorized access, intrusions, and suspicious behavior. Edge-based anomaly detection algorithms analyze sensor data locally to detect security threats and trigger alerts or automated responses to safeguard residents and property.

Edge computing and IoT are driving transformative innovations in machine learning, enabling real-time data processing, distributed intelligence, privacy-preserving learning, and enhanced security at the network edge. By harnessing the power of edge computing and IoT technologies, organizations can unlock new opportunities for intelligent automation, personalized services, and efficient resource utilization in various domains, including smart cities, industrial automation, healthcare, retail, and cybersecurity. As edge computing and

IoT continue to evolve, they will shape the future of machine learning by pushing intelligence closer to the data source and enabling seamless integration between edge and cloud environments for scalable and efficient ML applications.

Conclusion:

The future of machine learning promises exciting developments across various domains, driven by advancements in federated learning, continual learning, explainable AI, AutoML, reinforcement learning, and ethical AI practices. By embracing these trends and harnessing the potential of machine learning technologies, organizations can unlock new opportunities, address complex challenges, and drive innovation in the digital era. However, it's crucial to remain mindful of the ethical, societal, and regulatory considerations associated with AI adoption to ensure that machine learning technologies benefit humanity responsibly and ethically.

APPENDICES

1. Glossary of Terms:

The Glossary of Terms appendix serves as a comprehensive reference for readers to quickly access definitions and explanations of key terms, concepts, and acronyms used throughout the book. It enhances the reader's understanding of technical terminology and jargon specific to machine learning, ensuring clarity and consistency in communication. Here's an in-depth exploration of the Glossary of Terms appendix:

1. Definitions and Explanations:

- The glossary provides concise definitions and explanations for terms and concepts encountered in the book. Each entry is accompanied by a clear and understandable explanation that elucidates its meaning in the context of machine learning.

2. Key Terms and Concepts:

- The glossary covers key terms and concepts relevant to machine learning, including algorithms, models, techniques, metrics, and evaluation methods. It ensures readers have a solid grasp of fundamental concepts essential for understanding machine learning principles and practices.

3. Acronyms and Abbreviations:

- It includes acronyms and abbreviations commonly used in machine learning literature, ensuring readers can decipher shorthand notations and technical language without confusion. Each acronym is expanded to its full form, along with an explanation of its significance.

4. Organization and Accessibility:

- The glossary is organized alphabetically for easy navigation, allowing readers to quickly locate specific terms of interest. Entries are arranged in a structured format, making it convenient for readers to find definitions and explanations efficiently.

5. Cross-referencing:

- Cross-references may be included within the glossary to connect related terms and concepts, providing readers with additional context and insights. This enhances the reader's understanding of the interconnected nature of machine learning concepts and techniques.

6. Illustrative Examples:

- Some entries may include illustrative examples or use cases to further clarify the application and significance of specific terms or concepts. These examples help reinforce understanding and demonstrate how concepts are applied in real-world scenarios.

7. Updated and Expanded Content:

- The glossary may be periodically updated and expanded to incorporate new terms, concepts, and advancements in the field of machine learning. It reflects the evolving nature of the discipline and ensures that readers have access to the latest terminology and terminology.

8. Integration with Main Content:

- The glossary complements the main content of the book by providing readers with a comprehensive reference tool to reinforce learning and facilitate comprehension. It serves as a valuable resource for both novice and experienced practitioners seeking clarity on machine learning terminology.

The Glossary of Terms appendix is an indispensable resource that enhances the reader's understanding of machine learning concepts by providing clear and concise definitions, explanations, and examples. It serves as a valuable reference tool for readers to navigate complex terminology and technical language, ensuring clarity and consistency in communication throughout the book. By incorporating a comprehensive glossary, authors empower readers to deepen their understanding of machine learning principles and practices, fostering a more enriching and rewarding learning experience.

B. Python Code Snippets

Top of Form

`The Python Code Snippets appendix provides readers with practical examples of Python code relevant to the machine learning concepts discussed in the book. It serves as a hands-on reference for readers to understand, implement, and experiment with machine learning algorithms, techniques, and workflows using Python programming language. Here's an in-depth exploration of the Python Code Snippets appendix:

1. Code Examples for Machine Learning Algorithms:

- The appendix includes Python code snippets illustrating the implementation of various machine learning algorithms, such as linear regression, logistic regression, decision trees, random forests, support vector machines, k-nearest neighbors, and neural networks. Each code snippet is accompanied by comments explaining the purpose and functionality of the code.

2. Data Preprocessing and Feature Engineering:

- It provides code examples demonstrating data preprocessing techniques, such as data cleaning, handling missing values, feature scaling, encoding categorical variables, and feature extraction. These snippets showcase how to prepare raw data for machine learning model training and evaluation.

3. Model Evaluation and Hyperparameter Tuning:

- The appendix includes Python code snippets for model evaluation techniques, such as cross-validation, evaluation metrics, and hyperparameter tuning using techniques like grid search and random search. Readers can learn how to assess model performance, optimize model parameters, and fine-tune machine learning models for better results.

4. Visualization and Data Analysis:

- It offers code snippets for data visualization and exploratory data analysis using Python libraries like Matplotlib, Seaborn, and Pandas. Readers can visualize datasets, create plots, histograms, scatter plots, and heatmaps to gain insights into the underlying data distribution and relationships.

5. Integration with Machine Learning Libraries:

- The Python code snippets demonstrate how to leverage popular machine learning libraries and frameworks such as scikit-learn, TensorFlow, PyTorch, and Keras. Readers can see how to import these libraries, instantiate machine learning models, fit them to data, make predictions, and evaluate model performance.

6. Reproducibility and Experimentation:

- Code snippets in the appendix are designed to be reproducible, allowing readers to replicate experiments and results presented in the book. They serve as a foundation for readers to build upon and experiment with their own machine learning projects and applications.

7. Documentation and Best Practices:

- Each code snippet is accompanied by documentation and best practices for writing clean, efficient, and well-documented Python code. Readers can learn coding conventions, naming conventions, and software engineering principles for writing maintainable and scalable machine learning code.

8. Extensibility and Customization:

- The Python code snippets are modular and customizable, allowing readers to adapt them to their specific use cases, datasets, and requirements. Readers can extend the provided code to implement advanced features, custom algorithms, or novel machine learning techniques.

9. Community Engagement and Collaboration:

- The appendix encourages readers to engage with the broader machine learning community by sharing code snippets, seeking feedback, and collaborating on open-source projects. It fosters a culture of learning, collaboration, and knowledge sharing among machine learning practitioners.

10. Continuous Updates and Maintenance:

- The Python code snippets appendix may be periodically updated and maintained to incorporate new features, improvements, and advancements in machine learning libraries and frameworks. It ensures that readers have access to up-to-date code examples and resources.

The Python Code Snippets appendix serves as a valuable resource for readers to learn, practice, and experiment with machine learning concepts using Python programming language. It empowers readers to apply theoretical knowledge to real-world problems, develop practical skills in machine learning, and explore the vast landscape of machine learning algorithms and techniques. By providing clear, concise, and well-documented code examples, the Python Code Snippets appendix enhances the learning experience and facilitates the application of machine learning principles in practice.

C. Datasets for Practice:

The Datasets for Practice appendix provides readers with curated datasets that they can use to apply and reinforce the machine learning concepts discussed in the book. It serves as a valuable resource for hands-on learning, allowing readers to experiment with real-world data and gain practical experience in building and evaluating machine learning models. Here's an in-depth exploration of the Datasets for Practice appendix:

1. Curated Datasets:

- The appendix includes a selection of curated datasets spanning various domains, such as healthcare, finance, e-commerce, social media, and more. These datasets are carefully chosen to represent diverse data types, sizes, and complexities, catering to readers with different interests and skill levels.

2. Data Formats and Descriptions:

- Each dataset is accompanied by detailed descriptions, including information about the data source, format, features, and target variables. This helps readers understand the structure and characteristics of the data they are working with, enabling them to formulate research questions and hypotheses.

3. Preprocessing Guidelines:

- The appendix provides guidelines and recommendations for preprocessing the datasets, including steps for data cleaning, handling missing values, encoding categorical variables, and feature scaling. These guidelines help readers prepare the data for machine learning model training and evaluation.

4. Exploratory Data Analysis (EDA):

- Readers are encouraged to perform exploratory data analysis (EDA) on the datasets to gain insights into the data distribution, relationships, and patterns. The Datasets for Practice appendix may include code snippets or examples demonstrating how to visualize and analyze the data using Python libraries such as Pandas, Matplotlib, and Seaborn.

5. Model Training and Evaluation:

- Readers can use the datasets to train and evaluate machine learning models across various tasks, such as classification, regression, clustering, and more. The appendix may include code examples or tutorials illustrating how to instantiate machine learning models, fit them to data, make predictions, and evaluate model performance.

6. Benchmarking and Comparison:

- The datasets facilitate benchmarking and comparison of different machine learning algorithms and techniques. Readers can experiment with multiple models, parameter settings, and evaluation metrics to identify the most effective approaches for their specific use cases.

7. Real-world Applications:

- The datasets represent real-world scenarios and applications, allowing readers to tackle practical problems encountered in industry and academia. By working with authentic data, readers gain valuable insights into the challenges and complexities of applying machine learning in real-world contexts.

8. Community Engagement and Sharing:

- The Datasets for Practice appendix encourages readers to engage with the machine learning community by sharing their findings, insights, and experiences with the datasets. This fosters collaboration, knowledge sharing, and innovation among machine learning practitioners and enthusiasts.

9. Continuous Updates and Expansion:

- The appendix may be periodically updated and expanded to include new datasets, data sources, and challenges relevant to emerging trends and advancements in machine learning. This ensures that readers have access to a diverse and up-to-date collection of datasets for practice and experimentation.

The Datasets for Practice appendix serves as a valuable resource for readers to gain practical experience and proficiency in machine learning through hands-on learning with real-world data. By providing curated datasets, preprocessing guidelines, and model training examples, the appendix enables readers to apply and reinforce machine learning concepts in a practical and meaningful way. It empowers readers to explore, experiment, and innovate in the field of machine learning, fostering a deeper understanding and appreciation for the transformative potential of data-driven technologies.

D. Further Reading and Resources:

`The Further Reading and Resources appendix serves as a curated list of additional references, books, research papers, online courses, tutorials, and other resources to supplement the content covered in the book. It provides readers with opportunities to delve deeper into specific topics, explore advanced concepts, and broaden their understanding of machine learning. Here's an in-depth exploration of the Further Reading and Resources appendix:

1. Books:

- The appendix includes recommendations for books covering various aspects of machine learning, including introductory texts, advanced textbooks, specialized topics, and practical guides.

These books offer comprehensive coverage of machine learning concepts, algorithms, and applications, catering to readers with different levels of expertise and interests.

2. Research Papers and Journals:

- Readers are directed to seminal research papers, academic journals, and conference proceedings in the field of machine learning. These resources provide access to cutting-edge research, theoretical advancements, and innovative techniques developed by leading researchers and practitioners in academia and industry.

3. Online Courses and Tutorials:

- The appendix lists online courses, tutorials, and educational platforms offering interactive learning experiences in machine learning. These resources cover a wide range of topics, from basic concepts to advanced techniques, and provide learners with hands-on exercises, projects, and assessments to reinforce their understanding.

4. MOOCs and Specializations:

- Readers are provided with recommendations for massive open online courses (MOOCs) and specialization programs offered by renowned universities and educational institutions. These programs offer structured learning paths, video lectures, assignments, and quizzes, allowing learners to acquire valuable skills and credentials in machine learning.

5. Webinars and Workshops:

- The appendix highlights upcoming webinars, workshops, and conferences in the field of machine learning, where readers can engage with experts, participate in discussions, and stay updated on the latest trends and developments. These events provide opportunities for networking, collaboration, and knowledge sharing among machine learning professionals.

6. Online Communities and Forums:

- Readers are encouraged to join online communities, forums, and discussion groups focused on machine learning, such as Reddit, Stack Overflow, and GitHub. These platforms facilitate knowledge exchange, problem-solving, and peer support, allowing members to learn from each other's experiences and insights.

7. Blogs and Podcasts:

- The appendix includes recommendations for blogs, podcasts, and newsletters covering machine learning topics, trends, and industry updates. These resources offer valuable insights, expert opinions, and practical advice from leading practitioners and thought leaders in the field.

8. Open-source Libraries and Projects:

- Readers are directed to open-source machine learning libraries, frameworks, and projects hosted on platforms like GitHub. These repositories provide access to code samples, tutorials, documentation, and community contributions, enabling readers to explore, experiment, and contribute to open-source machine learning projects.

9. Online Datasets and Challenges:

- The appendix provides links to online repositories and platforms offering datasets, challenges, and competitions for machine learning research and practice. These resources allow readers to access curated datasets, participate in data science competitions, and benchmark their machine learning models against others in the community.

10. Industry Reports and Case Studies:

- Readers are provided with industry reports, case studies, and white papers showcasing real-world applications and success stories of machine learning in various industries, such as healthcare, finance, e-commerce, and technology. These resources offer insights into industry trends, best practices, and emerging use cases for machine learning.

The Further Reading and Resources appendix serves as a valuable guide for readers seeking to expand their knowledge, skills, and expertise in machine learning beyond the content covered in the book. By providing curated references, online courses, tutorials, and community resources, the appendix empowers readers to continue their learning journey, explore new topics, and stay updated on the latest advancements in the field of machine learning. It fosters a culture of lifelong learning, curiosity, and professional development among machine learning practitioners and enthusiasts.